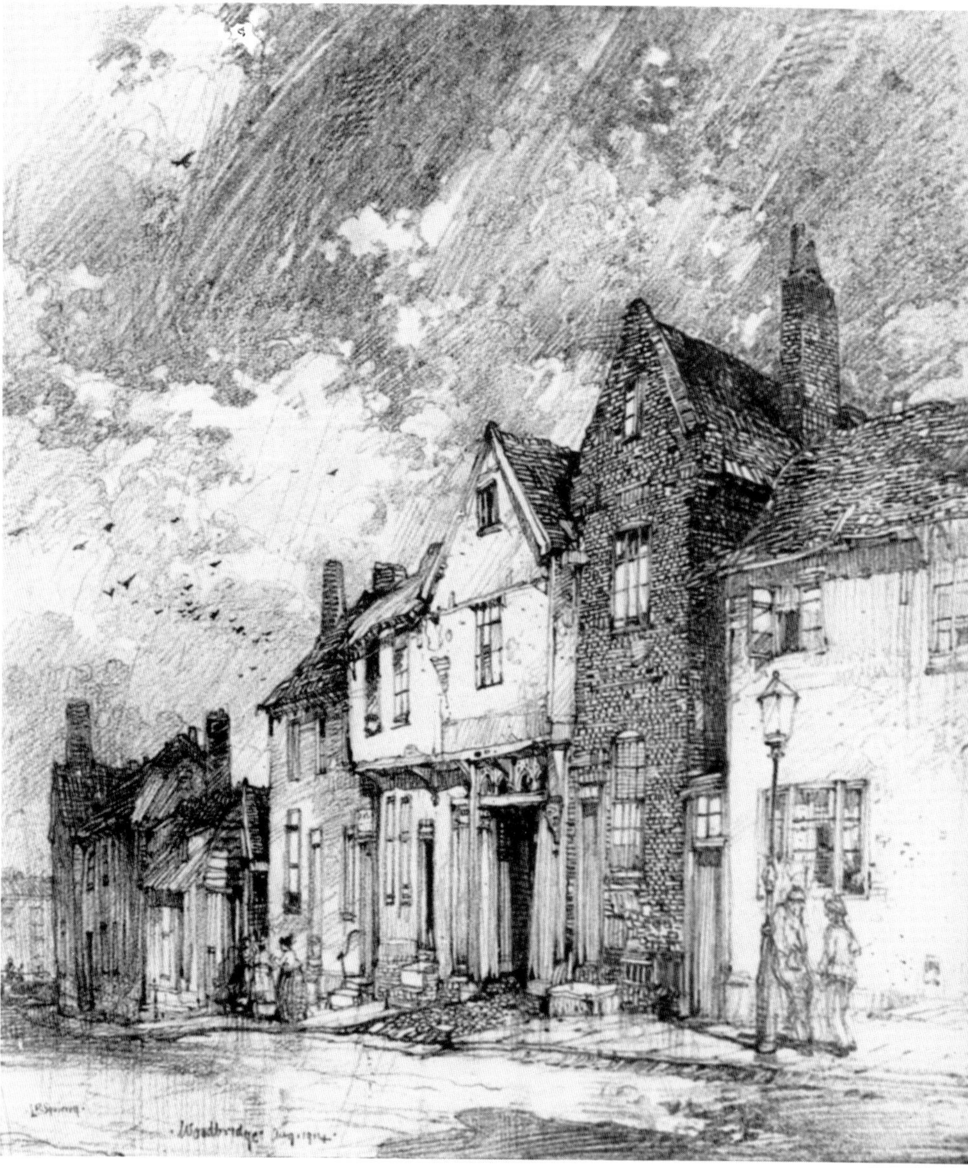

Old Houses, Woodbridge
Leonard Squirrell
(pencil drawing 1914)

Leonard Squirrell

R.W.S., R.E.

THE LAST OF THE NORWICH SCHOOL ?

Josephine Walpole

Published by
Antique Collectors' Club
5, Church Street, Woodbridge, Suffolk

ACKNOWLEDGEMENTS

As in my earlier books on Leonard Squirrell and his work, I acknowledge with grateful thanks the loyal support of his family and friends. Again I am also indebted to the Norfolk Museums Service, the Royal Watercolour Society, the Courtauld Institute, the Railway Museum, York, the East Anglian Daily Times, Andrew Casey and, perhaps most of all, to my indefatigable photographer, Peter Williams. As always, too, Antique Collectors' Club have shown the utmost care and patience with my whims.

While the majority of illustrations of Norwich School paintings are by courtesy of Norwich Castle Museum, others belong to individuals who prefer to remain anonymous and some I must confess to not knowing their present whereabouts, my collection of illustrations having extended over many years. The same could be said for some Squirrell illustrations although I am primarily indebted to his and my own family and friends. Others belong to anonymous owners to whom I extend my very grateful thanks. It is a sad fact of modern life that most private owners of valuable works of art who willingly permit their use for reproduction, feel obliged to keep secret their ownership; for the same reason, this author at least feels a double sense of appreciation and gratitude for their courtesy. In the public sector, as well as the Norwich source, the John Middleton is reproduced by courtesy of Trading Places International, the Squirrell painting of Angelsey Abbey trees by courtesy of the Fairhaven Collection, Anglesey Abbey (National Trust) and the cover illustration by courtesy of the Meadowlands Collection.

It will be understood that the illustrations in this book and earlier volumes by various authors represent only a small proportion of Leonard Squirrell's phenomenal output and a minute proportion of the collective works of the Norwich School painters, even of those mentioned. It is enough, however, to show the sharing of that intangible quality that binds together such a multiplicity of personalities, styles, media and interpretation that enables the perceptive onlooker to glance and say, 'Oh yes. . .Norwich School'.

J.W.

For Annette

CONTENTS

Introduction 9
1. The Norwich School 17
2. Watercolours of the Norwich School 27
3. The Common Denominator 49
4. The Cotman Connection 61
5. Reflections 88
6. Further 'Influences' 96
7. 'Squirrell is Different' 106

COLOUR ILLUSTRATIONS

The Blacksmith's Shop, Hingham, Norfolk,
John Crome 33

Hoveton Little Broad,
John Thirtle 36

Mildenhall Church from the Meadows,
Leonard Squirrell 37

Devon,
John Middleton 40

Trees near the Greta River,
John Sell Cotman 73

Stoke by Nayland,
Leonard Squirrell 76

St. Botolph's Priory, Essex,
John Sell Cotman, 76

Castle Acre Priory,
John Sell Cotman 77

Castle Acre Priory,
Leonard Squirrell 77

Haddiscoe Church,
Leonard Squirrell 80

Also 57 black and white illustrations

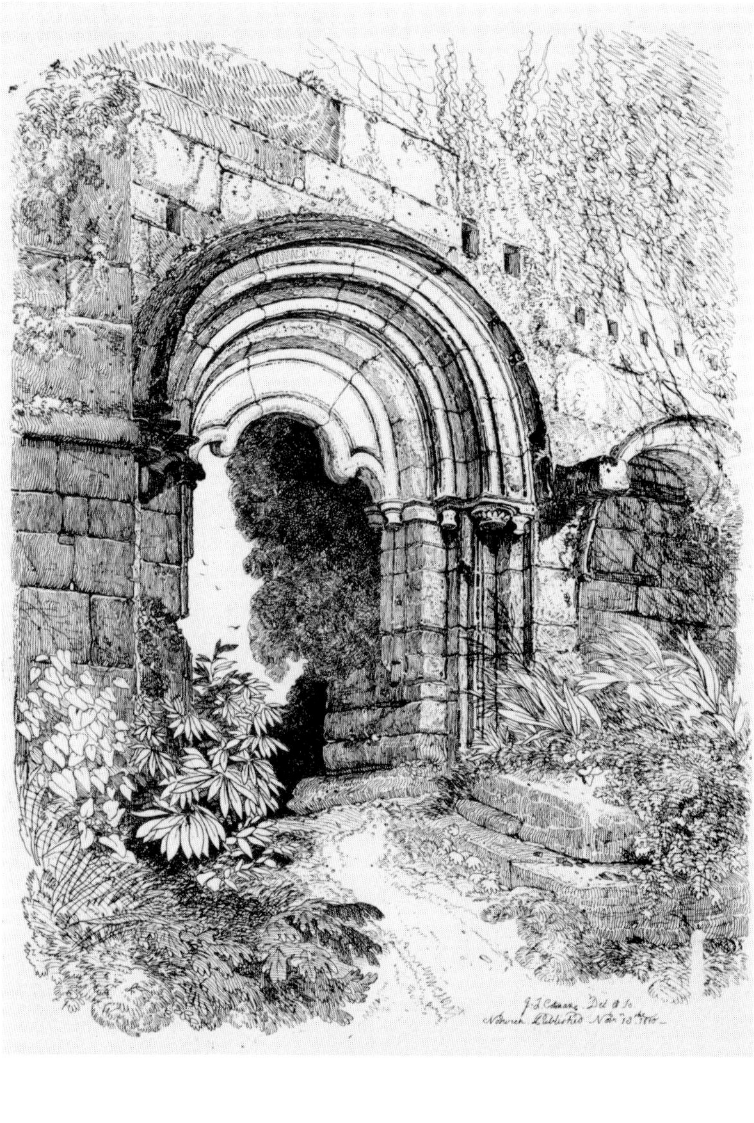

INTRODUCTION

Reflecting on a fourth Retrospective Exhibition ten years after Leonard Squirell's death, one was more than ever aware, not only of the accomplished professionalism of everything he did but of the personality aura, totally undiminished by the passage of time, that makes itself felt wherever and when ever his work is shown. One *sees* the paintings but, equally, *feels* the presence of their creator to the extent that it is often remarked how the prevailing atmosphere of his exhibitions becomes one of the peace and serenity reflected in both his character and his work. That Leonard Squirrell ranks with the immortals, already there is no shadow of doubt.

'Magic, that's what it is – sheer magic. . . .' So an elderly gentleman giving one last long look before reluctantly leaving the exhibition to which I have just referred.

I knew exactly what he meant for I and countless others have said it so many times. Magic is the only word one can find to describe the indefinable quality of Squirrell's work, a quality that overrides the accepted definition of the word even transcending the discipline and perfectionism of his craftsmanship.

In his lifetime, Squirrell was a modest, totally unassuming man who, despite the constant demand and the steady flow of commissions, never lost a certain childlike surprise and delight in the idea that anyone should genuinely want his work. To try and talk to him about his popularity or reputation simply occasioned something between a chuckle and a snort of utter disbelief and the coveted international awards received for his superb mezzotints were airily dismissed. Always generous with praise for others when he genuinely felt it was merited, he was his own sternest critic and would accept only the nearest thing to perfection from himself. So if perfection was his own criterion, why should people make a fuss just because someone had recognised and rewarded it? Engraving was an exacting craft and only acceptable to him, and therefore in his mind to others, if it fulfilled his own exacting standards. It has been said that humility is an essential ingredient of greatness – if this be so, Leonard Squirrell was truly great.

Perfection of execution can be cold and soulless but the warmth and sincerity that were so much part of his make up are ever present in Squirrell's work and always when a collection is shown, the atmosphere is charged with these qualities. There is, still, a conscious rapport between the artist and his faithful following – however much they may vie with each other for anything that is for sale! Somehow it is generally a friendly rivalry for always there is that intangible feeling of the artist's presence and wrangling was something foreign to him.

I mentioned earlier the extraordinary quality of Squirrell's work meaning, not its quality in terms of standard which speaks for itself, but an indefinable quality that sets him apart from any other contemporary artist, a charisma belonging to him alone. In some respects, perhaps, there is an affinity with certain of his peers particularly those who shared the discipline of the great Professor Tonks, but there are few living artists who can, to any significant extent, compare with the essential Squirrell.

The seemingly infinite variety within his etchings, engravings, watercolours, pastels and oils in both subject matter and approach, the ability to produce a Suffolk landscape which in colour and atmosphere could *only* be Suffolk but, equally sensitively, a scene in Italy or Southern France where the light, colour and warmth are so totally different could, in less capable hands, result in a loss of identity. Not so with Leonard Squirrell. From the quickest, spontaneous landscape sketch to a highly finished study of elaborate buildings or from the skilful, sophisticated mezzotint to a lively, delicate pastel – everything bears the unmistakeable Squirrell hallmark.

One of the most significant indications of this personal charisma and of the universal appeal of Squirrell, adding further proof that this is unlikely ever to diminish, is provided by the increasing number of young people who are not only interested in looking and studying the work of such a master but willing to pay high prices, often at some personal sacrifice, to own such treasures. One might expect his contemporaries, many of whom knew him well, and those of us who always appreciate the discipline and skill of the Tonks era, to be lost in respectful admiration coupled with nostalgia for his subjects and the age he represented, but young and old alike respond to the magic.

Take the young student with the punky hair-do, earring in one ear and three times oversized alpaca raincoat sporting a lady's cheap brooch on one lapel, who stood gazing.....

'I just hate traditional work normally, its so boring. It does nothing for me, I like something way out, exciting...except Squirrell. He's fantastic, absolutely incredible, he really gets to you...I'd give anything to own one.'

And true to his word even though after paying his lodgings he led a very frugal life, a minor windfall was immediately spent on a Squirrell working sketch, sold cheaply because of foxing and discolouration.

At the other end of the scale, take more than one well heeled young couple, 'yuppies,' probably still only in their twenties, who stayed on and on as if they could not bring themselves to go and then returned, again and again, totally fascinated by the quality, the skill, the magic . . . that eventually left them some hundreds of pounds poorer – or richer! Middle aged couples too, seemingly quite against their usual tastes, looking, talking, buying . . . elderly spinsters, youthful bachelors . . . From his own contemporaries to teenagers, even to the critics who frequently make a show of condemning the realistic, there was this extraordinarily consistent reaction.

Take the Indian doctor who had never previously heard of him – another race, another culture, but sufficiently impressed, not only to look with interest, but to buy. The American girl who had delightedly discovered an etching in a junk shop in the Midlands and wanted to see more. The young teacher who coveted a watercolour enough to tie herself to a year of monthly payments rather than let it go. The list could go on.

Eulogies can be boring and sometimes insincere; in this case the latter could not apply, the former I will not risk. In any event, to pretend actually to like everything Leonard Squirrell painted would be as disloyal to him as to ones own integrity. Like so many artists, thankfully to a lesser degree than his talented, underestimated contemporary, Vernon Ward, in the process of making a living he painted not a few uncongenial and boring commissioned subjects which had no particular appeal and it shows, even if only to those who knew him well. It has been said of John Sell Cotman that he was incapable of producing a bad drawing and the same sentiment could well be applied to Leonard Squirrell in terms of academic and technical excellence, but the real personal quality of any artist's work is most evident in that which he does for the love of it. As the years go by, as in the instance of Vernon Ward, the commercial commissions, the 'bread and butter' paintings, are forgotten and the 'real' work comes into its own.

It is the *real* Leonard Squirrell we are discussing here whose work I want more seriously, even if I cannot explain the magic, to analyse, and to assess, as I see it at this point of history, Squirrell's place in the world of East Anglian art. East Anglian art, in the eyes of the world outside, evolves around the Norwich School; it is interesting to consider the background that has occasioned the opinion now being expressed more and more frequently and by totally unconnected people, that in Squirrell we have 'the last of the Norwich School.'

Josephine Walpole
Woodbridge 1992

Artists belonging to or closely affiliated with the Norwich School

John Crome 1768-1821
Married Pheobe Burney, sister of Robert Ladbroke's wife

Robert Ladbroke 1769-1842
Married Pheobe Burney's sister Mary

John Berney Crome 1794-1842
Son and pupil of John Crome

William Henry Crome 1806-1866
Son of John Crome, pupil of John Berney Crome

Frederick John Crome 1796-1831

Emily Crome 1801-1840

John Berney Ladbroke 1803-1869
Son of Robert Ladbroke, pupil of John Crome

Henry Ladbroke 1800-1870
Son of Robert Ladbroke, pupil of John Crome

Frederick Ladbroke 1812-1865
Son of Robert Ladbroke

James Sillett 1764-1840 (Suffolk)

Emma Sillett fl. 1813-1833

James Stark 1794-1859
Pupil of John and John Berney Crome

John Sell Cotman 1782-1842

Miles Edmund Cotman 1810-1858
Son and pupil of John Sell Cotman – sometimes shared paintings

John Joseph Cotman 1814-1878
Son of John Sell Cotman

Frederick George Cotman 1850-1920
Nephew of John Sell Cotman

Henry Bright 1810-1873 (Suffolk)
Some teaching from John Sell Cotman and John Berney Crome, apprenticed to Alfred Stannard

Thomas Lound 1802-1861
Pupil of John Sell Cotman but more influenced by Crome, Stannard and Thirtle

John Thirtle 1777-1839
Brother-in-law of John Sell Cotman

Joseph Clover 1779-1853

Robert Leman 1799-1863

Robert Dixon 1780-1815

Anthony Sandys 1806-1883

Rev. Edward Thomas Daniell 1804-1842
Pupil John Crome, etched under Stannard

William Barnes Freeman 1813-1897
Pupil of John Sell Cotman

James Bulwer 1794-1879
Friend of the Cotmans

Joseph Geldart 1808-1882
Pupil of John Sell Cotman

C.H. Harrison 1842-1902

James Reeve 1833-1920
Pupil of John Berney Crome

Michael William Sharp 1801-1840
Lived with John Crome, studied under Sir William Beechey

Cornelius Jansen Walker Winter 1820-1891 (Suffolk)

Charles Catton, Jnr 1756-1819
Studied under father, Charles Catton, R.A.

William Capon 1757-1827

William Williams fl.1758-1795

George Clint 1770-1854

Daniel Coppin 1771-1822

Henry Jutsum 1816-1869
Pupil of James Stark

H.B. Love 1800-1838

E. Bell
Founder member of the Norwich Society, pupil of Charles Hodgson

Maria Margetson 1832-1896
Niece of John Berney Ladbroke Pupil of Eloise Stannard

Joseph Paul 1804-1887

John Paul
Son of Joseph Paul, dates unknown

Henry Walton 1746-1813
Norfolk 'School' rather pre-Norwich School but often considered with them

Edwin Cooper 1785-1833 (Suffolk)
Pupil of Marshall, painted with John Crome

Joseph Stannard 1797-1830
Pupil of Robert Ladbroke

Alfred Stannard 1806-1889
Brother of Joseph Stannard, possibly pupil of John Crome

Alfred George Stannard 1828-1915
Son of Alfred Stannard, also pupil

Eloise Harriet Stannard 1829-1915
Daughter and pupil of Alfred Stannard

Emily Stannard (Mrs Joseph) 1803-1885

John Middleton 1827-1856
Pupil of John Berney Ladbroke and Henry Bright

George Vincent 1764-1840
Pupil of John Crome

Arthur James Stark 1831-1902
Son and pupil of James Stark

Alfred Priest 1810-1850
Pupil of Henry Ninham and James Stark

Samuel David Colkett 1800-1863
Pupil of James Stark

Victoria Colkett fl. 1858-68
Daughter and pupil of S.D. Colkett

John Ninham 1754-1817

Henry Ninham 1793-1874
Son of John Ninham

Charles Hodgson c.1770-1856
Friend of Crome and Ladbrook

David Hodgson 1798-1864
Son of Charles Hodgson. Pupil of John Crome

William Joy 1803-1867

John Cantiloe Joy 1806-1866
Brother of William Joy

Obadiah Short 1803-1886

Mrs Dawson-Turner 1774-1850
Pupil of John Sell Cotman

Elizabeth Turner 1799-1852
Pupil of John Sell Cotman

Mary Anne Turner 1803-1874
Pupil of John Sell Cotman

John Varley 1778-1842

Cornelius Varley 1781-1873

Chapter 1

THE NORWICH SCHOOL

'There is a deep, unconscious bond between them, so that many a painting, though we may be at a loss to attribute it to a particular artist, is immediately recognised as belonging to the Norwich School.'

Lawrence Binyon.

Within all major schools of painting every artist is also an individual and Leonard Squirrell was always his own man. At the same time, one becomes more and more aware of the bridging of the time span and the truth of the now widely held belief that in Squirrell we have 'the last of the Norwich School.'

However, before discussing any special relationship between the two, we must first consider in a general way the School itself and the work of some of its best known painters. Undoubtedly the Norwich School is by far the most important school of painting to have developed in nineteenth century Britain, in fact many experts agree that it is the only true example of a provincial school of painting. One art historian in particular makes much of a Suffolk school of painting but it is debatable whether the painters included,* all famous or prestigious artists in their own individualistic right, consitute a school in the same sense. I quote John Constable: 'The writers of Art employ the word school to denote a similarity of feeling and practice in many individuals arising from the example of one powerful individual yet by no means implying a want of originality in the rest. In Painting, so many areas of excellence are open, that every painter of fame is distinguished from the rest by some perfection which is to be found with himself only.'

The painters of the Norwich School worked with an unequalled degree of consistent individual and collective professionalism which has not only stood the test of time but grown in stature and importance over the years. While other so called schools have come and gone, provincial though it may be in a literal sense, there is nothing parochial about the Norwich School, now nationally and internationally collectable – at a price!

The Norwich Society, regarded as the forerunner of the Norwich School of Painters, was formed in 1803 although, in a sense, the

Norwich School had its beginnings around 1790 when John Crome's apprenticeship ended and he, with Robert Ladbroke (1769-1842), began it all. Although it is generally assumed that the greatest painters of the Norwich School died out towards the end of the nineteenth century, there are certain worthy successors who should not be ignored. Equally some lesser painters of the early Norwich School are now coming into their own and being totally accepted as 'belonging' while a number of Suffolk artists, Bright, Sillett, Cooper and others, are important members of the School.

It is universally recognised that John Crome the elder (1768-1821) was the founder of the Norwich School whose collective identity was established through the Norwich Society of Artists founded as aforementioned in 1803 by Crome and Ladbroke. They were followed by Robert Dixon (1780-1815), John Thirtle (1777-1839), Charles Hodgson (1770-1856), James Stark (1794-1859) and, a little later, John

* The painters listed below have, by some authorities, been classed as the Suffolk School. I feel, however, that excellent and well known artists as most of them are, they lack the coherence of the Norwich School and are far too individualistic, each in his own right, actually to be regarded as a school.

Thomas Gainsborough	1727-1788
George Frost	1744-1821
Gainsborough Dupont	1755-1797
John Constable	1776-1837
Edward Ladell	1781-1886
John Dunthorne, Jnr.	1798-1832
Thomas Churchyard	1798-1868
Robert Burrows	1810-1883
E.R. Smythe	1810-1899
John Duvall	1816-1892
Henry George Alken	1816-1894
John Moore	1820-1902
Edwin Edwards	1823-1879
Thomas Smythe	1825-1906
George Thomas Rope	1845-1929
Henry George Todd	1846-1898
J. Sheppard	fl.1878-1899
Christopher Mark Mascall	1846-1933

Sell Cotman (1782-1842) when he returned to the City in 1806. Crome, Cotman, Ladbroke and Hodgson all had sons who inherited their fathers' artistic talents while Crome and Ladbroke both took pupils. In this way a second generation of the Norwich School was born, all influenced by their fathers and fathers' peers but all with their own share of original ideas and creativity. John Berney Crome (1794-1842) and W.H. Crome (1806-1866), Henry, John Berney and Fred Ladbroke (1800-1870, 1803-1879 and 1812-1865), Miles Edmund and John Joseph Cotman (1810-1848 and 1814-1878), Joseph (1797-1830) and a succession of Stannards, George Vincent and other pupils were part of this second generation. In their turn they were followed by the later Stannards, Henry Bright (1810-1873), Thomas Lound (1802-1861), John Middleton (1827-1856) and others, each with his own individuality but also taking from his forebears, and so the descent continued.

The Norwich Society's first Exhibition was held in 1805 and with the exception of 1826 and 27 annual Exhibitions followed. Intermarriage between families (for instance, Robert Ladbroke married the sister of Pheobe Berney who had married John Crome) created even stronger ties than the love of art and the Norwich School went from strength to strength. Crome, Cotman and other senior members had some influential patrons; enthusiasm for the arts in Norwich ran very high and Norwich itself was regarded as one of the country's foremost cultural centres. Many of the leading Norwich painters exhibited regularly in London where their names became increasingly familiar and their reputations stretched well beyond the Norfolk boundaries.

Thanks to the number of pupils and followers who copied and emulated his work, original John Cromes need careful identification today and are quite hard to find. In many ways the senior Crome, who ranks with Constable and Turner as one of the foremost landscape painters of his time, owes much to the influence of the Dutch 17th century masters particularly Ruisdael, Cuyp and Hobbema; the influence of Gainsborough is also evident, not unnaturally as Gainsborough was probably one of the first British artists to forge the strong link between the painters of Holland and East Anglia. Crome's work is more direct than that of Gainsborough who often worked in a somewhat fanciful way as opposed to the former's painting directly from nature, faithfully and truthfully, at the same time skilfully evoking the atmosphere of the Norfolk countryside while giving the whole work his own individual character whatever the source of early influence.

Although over the years any repetitive influence gradually wore away, his sons and pupils and certain of his most devoted followers produced some excellent work of their own albeit in some cases almost indistinguishable from that of the elder Crome to those who were (and are) not totally familiar with certain very personal nuances. It is Crome's brushwork that identifies him, in fact 'brushwork' is hardly the right expression here for Crome tended more to 'place' on his paint, his exceptional feeling for tonal value and harmony giving the resulting glow so characteristic of his work. His intensive study of the Dutch masters, too, must have further influenced his polished technique. There were bad 'imitations,' of course, but Ladbroke, Stark and his own sons, though not necessarily aware of the extent to which some of their earlier works might *appear* as copies, were excellent painters in their own right and as their personalities developed their work gained in interest and individual quality.

His co-founder of the Norwich Society, Robert Ladbroke, also worked primarily in oils in a rather heavy, Dutch inspired style, his early work having a distinct relationship to that of John Crome although his colours were darker and more sombre. He also painted a large number of on the spot oil sketches of which few seem to have survived but which had a certain spontaneity more appealing than his finished work. His watercolours and drawings, too, are virtually non-existent now but those recorded suggest that his draughtsmanship was weaker than Crome's and that all of his painting was considerably less sophisticated. He was later to be completely outshone by his third son, John Berney Ladbroke, 1800-1869, whose work showed a superior understanding of tone and colour together with a more sensitive brushwork. He also turned out some extremely gifted pupils notably John Middleton and Joseph Stannard, 1797-1830, who, after Crome and Cotman, was one of the most distinguished painters working in Norwich. The Dutch influence again is strong in Stannard's work but his skilful use of light gives the work a brighter, more lively, feeling and, despite his meticulous attention to detail, a touch of poetry.

Of John Crome's sons, the best known is John Berney (Moonlight) Crome, 1794-1842. Blessed with a somewhat precocious talent, John Berney, under the influence and teaching of his father, was painting in oils at the age of twelve and exhibiting paintings, oils and watercolours, for sale by the time he was seventeen. The Norwich

Mercury wrote of him, '. . . he emulates the industry and promises to surpass the talents of his father, for he is trained to art by a liberal education.' In 1819 he was made President of the Norwich Society, something of an honour for one so young, and after his father's death he took over the teaching practice with which he had assisted for some years. Few people are not familiar with his seemingly interminable moonlight scenes (between 1806 and 1833 he is known to have produced over seventy!) but his talent was much broader than is often realised. It was said in his youth that the promise he showed might well make him a greater painter than his father but, sadly, his work became uneven later in life no doubt as a result of ill health, financial problems and alchohol. William Henry (1806-1866) is, on the other hand, sadly underrated. While his earlier work is undoubtedly influenced by his father and elder brother, he developed a very personal, very beautiful colour sense and some of his skies are outstanding examples of their unique East Anglian quality.

In no way could John Sell Cotman (1782-1842) be called a follower of Crome in the artistic sense although he in his turn had his pupils and imitators. To my mind he is the most outstanding of the Norwich School painters and was certainly greatly admired by Leonard Squirrell and his contemporaries. It may be that the feeling for good drawing and watercolour that I share with Leonard Squirrell has some influence here but, again, these are the media with which in this discussion we shall be primarily concerned. Always recognised as a superb draughtsman, which, after all, is the common denominator of every real work of art, the breadth of Cotman's talent was never fully appreciated in his lifetime. Fifty or more years on with the advent of the impressionists and a more openminded approach, the more perceptive or intuitive follower of the visual arts realised that he had, quite simply, been years ahead of his time.

Undoubtedly influenced by Turner and Girtin, Cotman's personality and talent would have stood up on its own without any outside associations whatsoever. A temperamental, rather unsettled, individual, Cotman travelled a great deal both in this country and abroad but, wherever he was, his work took on the atmosphere of the environment as well as being a skilful representation of whatever landscape, architecture or other subject he or his influentual patrons desired. John Sell Cotman worked in a number of different styles and media, his mercurial temperament and grasshopper mind leading him to experiment and innovate invariably with successful results. It has been said that Cotman was incapable of producing a bad drawing and this is absolute fact – his architectural draughtsmanship has no equal and the drawings produced for his patron, Dawson Turner, during the Normandy period are some of the most accomplished of all time.

His restless disposition and moods varying from almost manic depression to a gay, abandoned charm inevitably produced a varied pattern of work but only an artist of Cotman's exceptional skill could hope to maintain a consistent standard throughout all the variations. On a purely personal plane, there are instances where his strength of colour is quite hard to accept but that is not to underestimate the overall quality and assurance of his work. Riotous, full bodied blue and gold tones alternate with subtle, almost monotonal, masterpieces of simplification yet, as opposed to Crome and his immediate followers, it is hard not to be sure of the identity of a John Sell Cotman – except possibly in those works shared with one of his sons! Robert Ladbroke's son, Henry, once wrote, '. . . as a man of genius, Cotman was much Crome's superior.' The young man, it would seem, was more forward looking than most of his generation.

* * * * * * * * * * * * * * *

John Crome, Robert Ladbroke and John Sell Cotman followed by their sons, pupils and apprentices, between them produced a varied and variable spectrum of work but they remain the foundation on which the Norwich School was firmly built. To those who followed they have bequeathed something in the nature of a family tree, each character that followed reflecting his own personality in his painting while retaining always some of the magic that had been handed down.

While Crome's influence speaks loudest through his own and Ladbroke's sons, James Stark (1794-1859), George Vincent (1796-1836) and his sons, probably the artists most influenced by Cotman were Robert Dixon (1780-1815) and John Thirtle (1779-1839), both Norwich men. Thirtle, a (London trained) Norwich picture framer, was also a founder member of the Norwich Society and Cotman's brother-in-law although little is known of him in that connection. Initially he exhibited portraits, often miniatures, at the Norwich Society's Exhibitions but later became interested in landscape, producing some of the finest watercolours of the era. His sense of atmosphere was particularly strongly developed and his handling of the broad wash technique developed by John Sell Cotman showed great confidence and skill. Dixon was a talented scene painter who worked at the Norwich Theatre and also taught drawing. Drawing was indeed his strong point for his sketches show a vitality considerably less evident in his pure watercolours of which only a few survive. Others which could more correctly be called coloured drawings, have all the quality of good draughtsmanship that made him an excellent artist in his own particular idiom.

As well as being a pupil of Crome, James Stark studied at the Royal Academy Schools and was a particularly prolific artist despite recurring ill health. The influence of Crome and the Dutch artist Hobbema are evident in much of his work. Although today his work commands high prices, and his patrons included such famous names as the Marquis of Stafford, Sir John Grey Egerton, the Countess de Gray, Lord Northwich and the academicians Thomas Phillips, Francis Chastney and Sir George Beaumont, I personally feel that George Vincent was Crome's most outstanding pupil. His work, although primarily in oil, had all the lightness and breadth so well suited to East Anglian subjects.

Joseph Stannard's is another name familiar to most people irrespective of their interest in the Norwich School as such. He became a pupil of Ladbroke although with his exceptional talent, he could only have made an exceptional painter. Initially he worked primarily on portrait subjects but soon branched into the landscapes with which we are most familiar. Possibly a year spent in Holland studying and painting the Dutch rivers influenced both his subject matter and style, certainly the influence of the Dutch masters comes through in much of his work. He was a fine engraver too as might be expected from his perfectionist style and virtuosity. He not only married the still life painter, Emily Coppins, but produced a talented daughter, another Emily.

His brother Alfred who subsequently taught drawing in Norwich, was one of his pupils along with the Reverend E.T. Daniell (1804-1842), a fine draughtsman known most widely for his well crafted etchings. Alfred Stannard's work, while retaining his brother's influence, is slightly artificial and over stylised although his watercolours, making use of very pure washes, have a personality all of their own. His son, Alfred G. Stannard, travelled extensively and his ability to absorb the atmosphere of a place coupled with a certain dramatic skill made him a much livelier painter than his father. His sister, Eloise, who probably studied with her cousin Emily, became a still life painter of exceptional beauty and skill.

John Berney Ladbroke's niece, Maria Margitson (1830-1896), who is said to have studied with Eloise Harriet Stannard, was another excellent still life painter. With Edwin Cooper (1785-1833), a Suffolk painter of equestrian subjects who exhibited primarily with the Norwich Society and gained his most prestigious commissions in Norfolk, the lady Stannards and Miss Margitson are probably the only Norwich School painters to have deviated totally from the landscape tradition although nationally and internationally they are some of its most important artists. James Sillett (1764-1840) painted still life as well as landscape, likewise his daughter, Emma Sillett, and Joseph Clover (1779-1853) was primarily a portrait painter giving the lie to those who think of the Norwich School in terms of (largely East Anglian) traditional landscapes.

Another Suffolk artist of the Norwich School, Henry Bright (1810-1853), was apprenticed for a time to a Woodbridge chemist. While still continuing with this work, he took painting lessons from John Berney Crome and went on to become an extremely successful artist. He had a completely natural talent and feeling for both draughtsmanship and colour and his dexterity of hand and clever use of light make his work, particularly some of his earlier painting, some of the most outstanding of the School. His friends, Thomas Lound and John Middleton, were both able painters, Lound rather following the Cotman tradition in his watercolours while Middleton who was first taught by John Berney Ladbroke, had a talent and style all of his own. Sadly his legacy of work is all too small for his premature death at the age of twenty nine robbed the Norwich School, indeed the whole world of art, of an exceptionally brilliant painter.

* *

It will be understood that this is but a brief summary of the Norwich School and that, included in or involved with the School, there are many other artists of great merit in addition to the more familiar names I have touched on here. In the next chapter I shall be discussing in further detail the watercolours and watercolour painters of the Norwich School for, in relating Leonard Squirrell to the School, watercolours, together with drawings and etchings, are of particular importance. Leonard Squirrell occasionally painted in oils and, as in every medium he attempted, produced some very fine work although it was not a medium he cared for and he rarely used it from choice. Watercolour was his first and greatest love with good drawing as the common denominator for everything while, above all, the Norwich tradition of dedication and sincerity shone through every facet of his work.

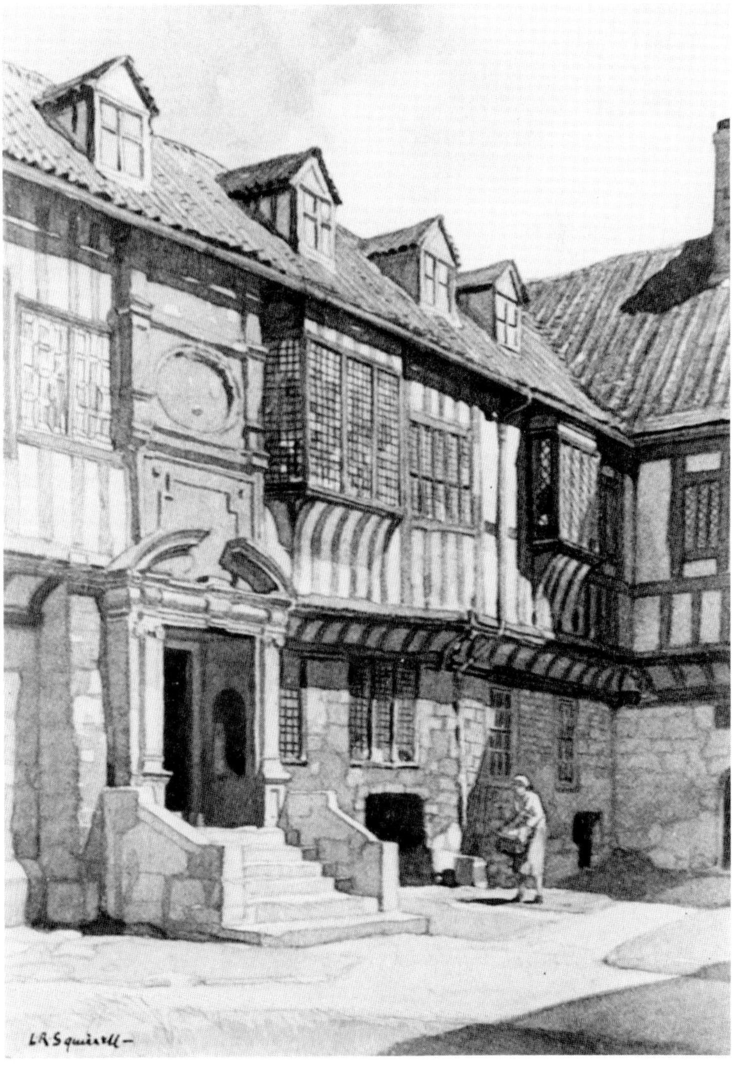

Courtyard, St. William's College, York Leonard Squirrell (watercolour c.1930)

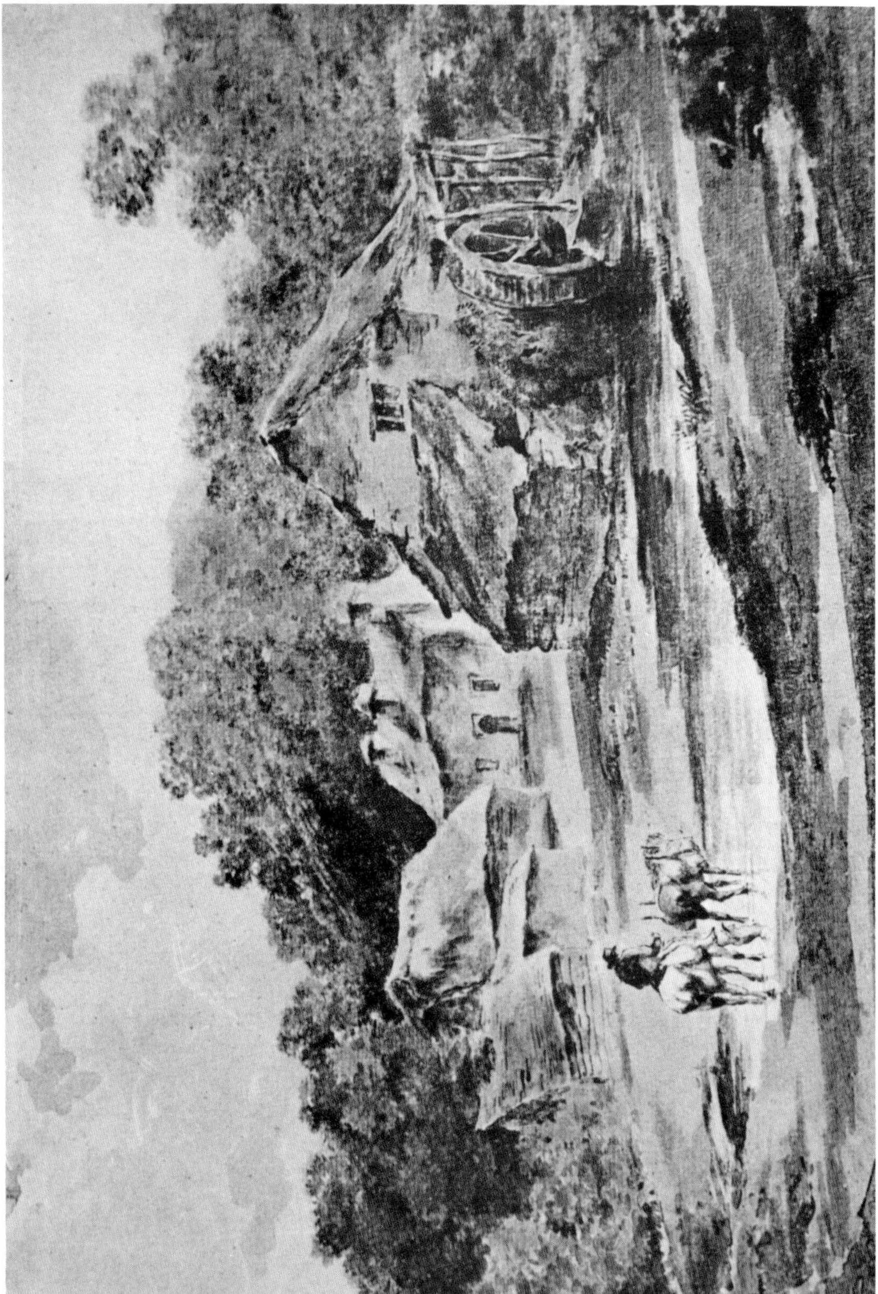

The Mill Wheel
John Crome (watercolour c.1795)

Chapter 2

WATERCOLOURS OF THE NORWICH SCHOOL

The only watercolourist of the Norwich School to have, on his own admission, influenced Leonard Squirrell's work is John Sell Cotman. Others, consciously or unconsciously, may have done so to a degree but this can only be conjecture. For this reason, I am omitting John Sell Cotman from this chapter in order firstly to explore the more, as it were, accidental relationships.

John Crome was not a watercolourist as such but his importance as co-founder of the Norwich Society, subsequently the Norwich School, demands that we at least consider his work in the medium. The interesting connection here between Crome and Squirrell is that, going backwards in time, one notices the influence of Girtin on both. This influence seems to permeate all Crome's known watercolours particularly, perhaps, his monochrome works such as 'Whitlingham' and 'Near Lakenham' in the Norwich Castle Museum. They identify with a Squirrell monochrome of my own although here the influence is unashamedly Cotman, unconsciously Girtin. With a few exceptions, Crome's watercolours could equally have been oils, the approach and the subject matter is so similar – the most notable exception is the early (c.1795) 'The Mill Wheel' which has a freshness and purity rather lacking in his later work in the medium. 'The Blacksmith's Shop at Higham' although undated also retains this early freshness and is the only other work I have seen reproduced which has this essentially watercolour quality.

Although influenced by both Crome and John Sell Cotman, John Thirtle's work could never be the victim of mistaken identity and having passed through a period of rather mediocre portraits into the realm of architectural and landscape studies, proved himself to be one of the most important watercolourists of the Norwich School. By trade he was a picture framer in Norwich and a number of his frames are known still to exist. His business as well as his painting brought him into close contacts with most of the local artists of the time and it was through his friendship with John Sell Cotman that he met and married the latter's wife's sister.

Thirtle's work can almost be divided into two periods, prior to 1817 when he stopped exhibiting for a time, probably owing to pressure

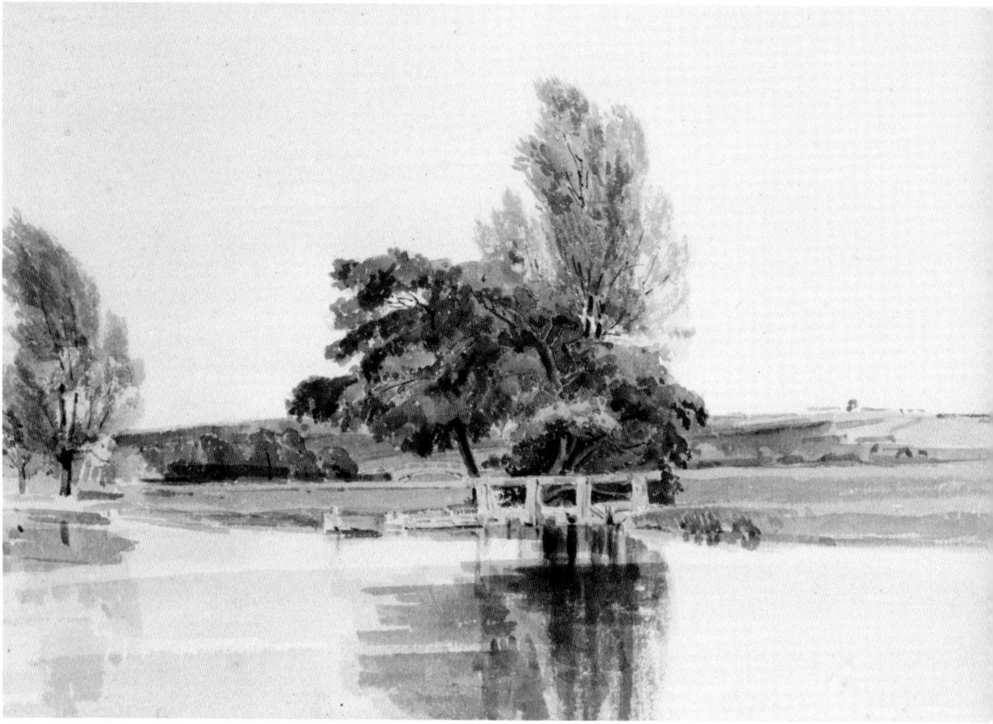

Riverside Scene near Norwich
John Thirtle
(watercolour)

both of business and ill health, and during the years between 1828 and 1830. When he had no work to show in the 1818 annual Exhibition of the Norfolk and Norwich Society of Artists, the Norwich Mercury commented significantly, 'We lament exceedingly that Mr Thirtle should not have found time for a single drawing. His occupation is doubly to be regretted because he stands highest and alone in the particular and beautiful department of watercolours, in which he has evinced so much decided excellence.' Some say that he peaked in 1814-1817 but the later period saw the production of some very fine works which show a tremendous feeling for atmosphere as well as being beautifully drawn and sympathetically observed. He was always particularly accomplished with almost monotone studies, probably his main link with Crome, and the judicious use of pencil was a feature of most of his earlier works. It was the influence of Cotman, no doubt, that encouraged him occasionally to use interesting variations of stronger colours between 1812 and 1817 but, unlike Cotman, he

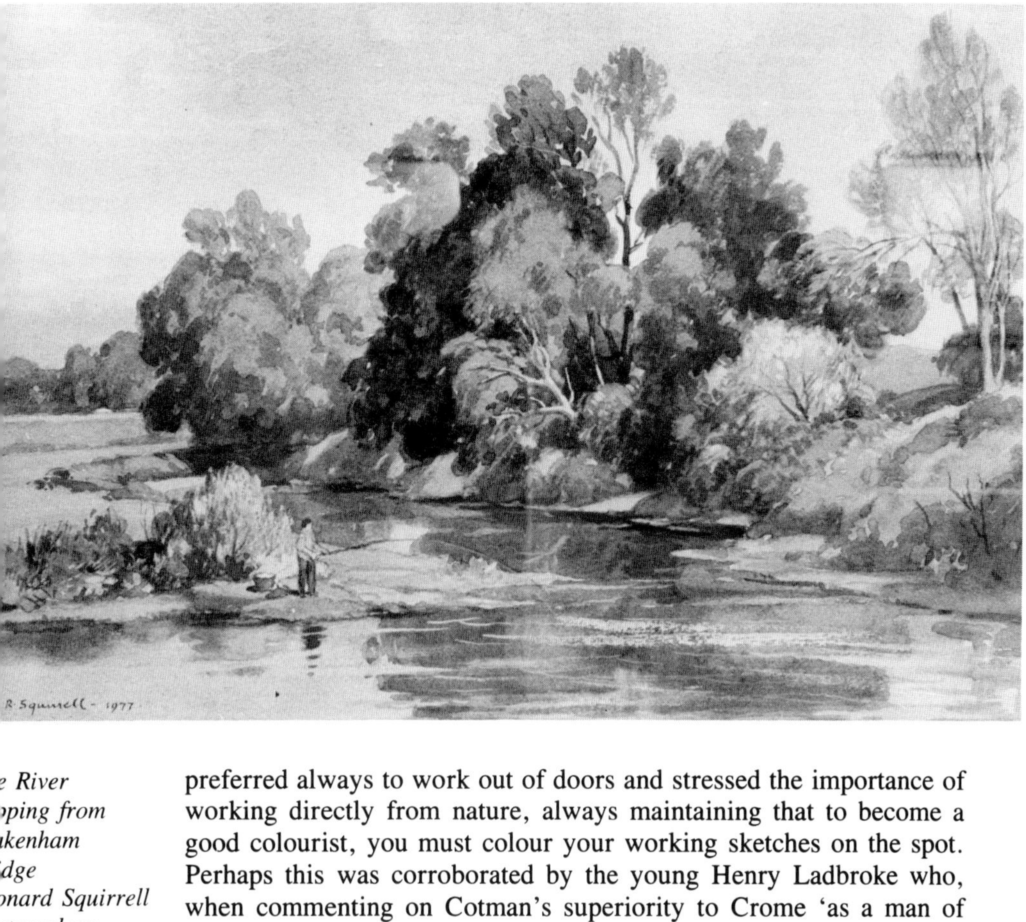

e River
pping from
ikenham
idge
onard Squirrell
atercolour
77)

preferred always to work out of doors and stressed the importance of working directly from nature, always maintaining that to become a good colourist, you must colour your working sketches on the spot. Perhaps this was corroborated by the young Henry Ladbroke who, when commenting on Cotman's superiority to Crome 'as a man of genius,' added 'and as a colourist Thirtle far surpasses them both.'

In his foreword to Marjorie Allthorpe-Guyton's book on Thirtle, Frances Cheetham writes, 'Although John Thirtle is one of the best of the Norwich School artists, he has remained one of the less well known and his place among early English watercolourists has yet to be fully appreciated.' The author herself writes, 'There is no more shadowy and elusive figure among the artists of the Norwich School than John Thirtle. He was, next to Crome and Cotman, the most talented watercolourist of his generation yet little is known of his life...' Thankfully, at last, this situation seems to be changing; while there is still a long way to go, more and more is John Thirtle being recognised

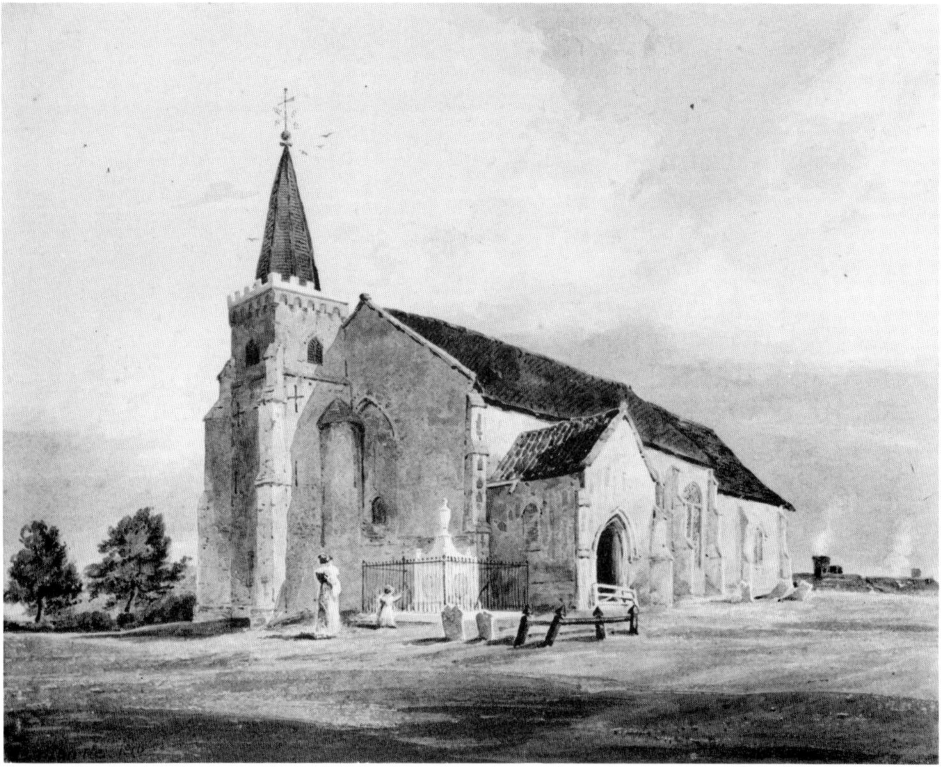

St. Edmund's Church, Costessey, Norfolk
John Thirtle (watercolour 1816)

as the unassuming genius he undoubtedly was. One again thinks of Leonard Squirrell but, somehow, I feel that posterity will not have so long to wait.

Thirtle obviously enjoyed painting river scenes, often with bridges, and broadland views with wherries are very predominant although, as he painted very little outside Norwich and Norfolk, this might be expected. He was also very much at home with buildings and city corners, particularly outstanding examples being 'Tombland' (Ill.), 'Haymarket, Norwich,' and his many churches, notably 'St. Mary's, Wroxham.' He shares with Leonard Squirrell the ability to make an interesting, beautifully composed picture of a totally unremarkable corner that appealed to him, and the impeccable drawing of both artists would give life and vitality to the most prosaic subjects.

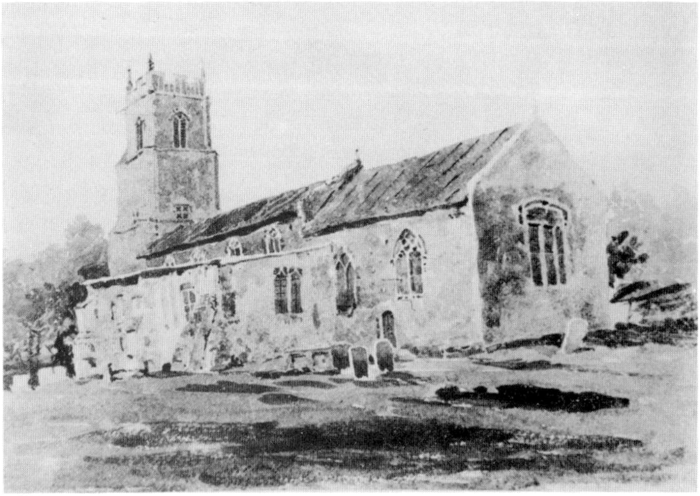

St. Mary's Church, Wroxham
John Thirtle
(watercolour and pencil c.1814)

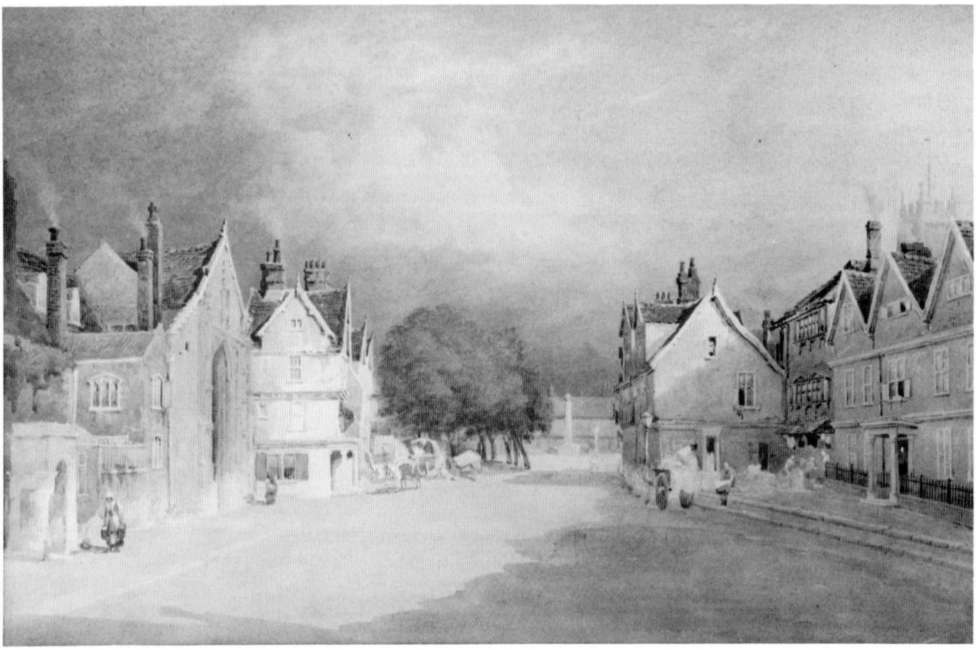

Tombland, Norwich
John Thirtle (watercolour)

It seems apparent that Thirtle felt great satisfaction, especially in his more highly finished works, with the use of near monochrome, often using tones of a beautifully warm sienna, perhaps one of the most accomplished being 'Boat Builder's Yard near the Cow Tower, Norwich', which has fine detail without clutter and, as always, an almost haunting sense of atmosphere. Thankfully, this work is well preserved but, in many others, where he has used a particularly fugitive blue (probably the destructive indigo so popular at that time) in his skies and in some of the greys, this has succumbed to light and upset the delicate tonal balance so characteristic of this artist's work. As with John Sell Cotman, one feels that Thirtle was often well ahead of his time, particularly in some of his watercolour sketches which have the charm and looseness of a much later period and in the main are lively little studies. An excellent example, also of his occasional use of strong colour, is 'Hoveton Little Broad' c.1815-20. The warm colourwashed cottages positively glow in the evening light against the dull olive of the trees with splashes of ochre light; by contrast in 'Riverside Scene, near Norwich' he uses Cotman's broad wash technique in tones of green and grey with highlights that almost sparkle. Then there are such gloriously free studies as 'The Abbot's Bridge, Bury St. Edmunds' and 'Pitch's Boathouse, opposite Cow Tower, Norwich', which are almost modern in conception, and one particular little wherry scene in pencil and wash is flavoured with Ivon Hitchens.

I make no apology for lingering on John Thirtle – I find his work exceptional and, although Leonard Squirrell never mentioned him to me, there is a close natural affinity which makes him particularly relevant to this present discussion. I have the feeling, too, that there may well have been some personal affinity; there is a lot to be learned of character through painting and here I sense two kindred souls. For a time Henry Ladbroke was a pupil of Thirtle and, like Martin Hardie nearly a hundred and fifty years later, expressed the view that Thirtle was a greater artist than Crome. Also, in perfect truth, 'As long as art is admired and studied, the watercolour drawings of Thirtle will be held in the highest esteem.'

James Stark (1794-1859), a pupil of John Crome, ranks fairly high in importance as a watercolourist of the Norwich School although his best known works are executed in oil. He was a contemporary of John Berney Crome at the Norwich Grammar School and was articled to the latter's father in 1811. From there he progressed to the Royal

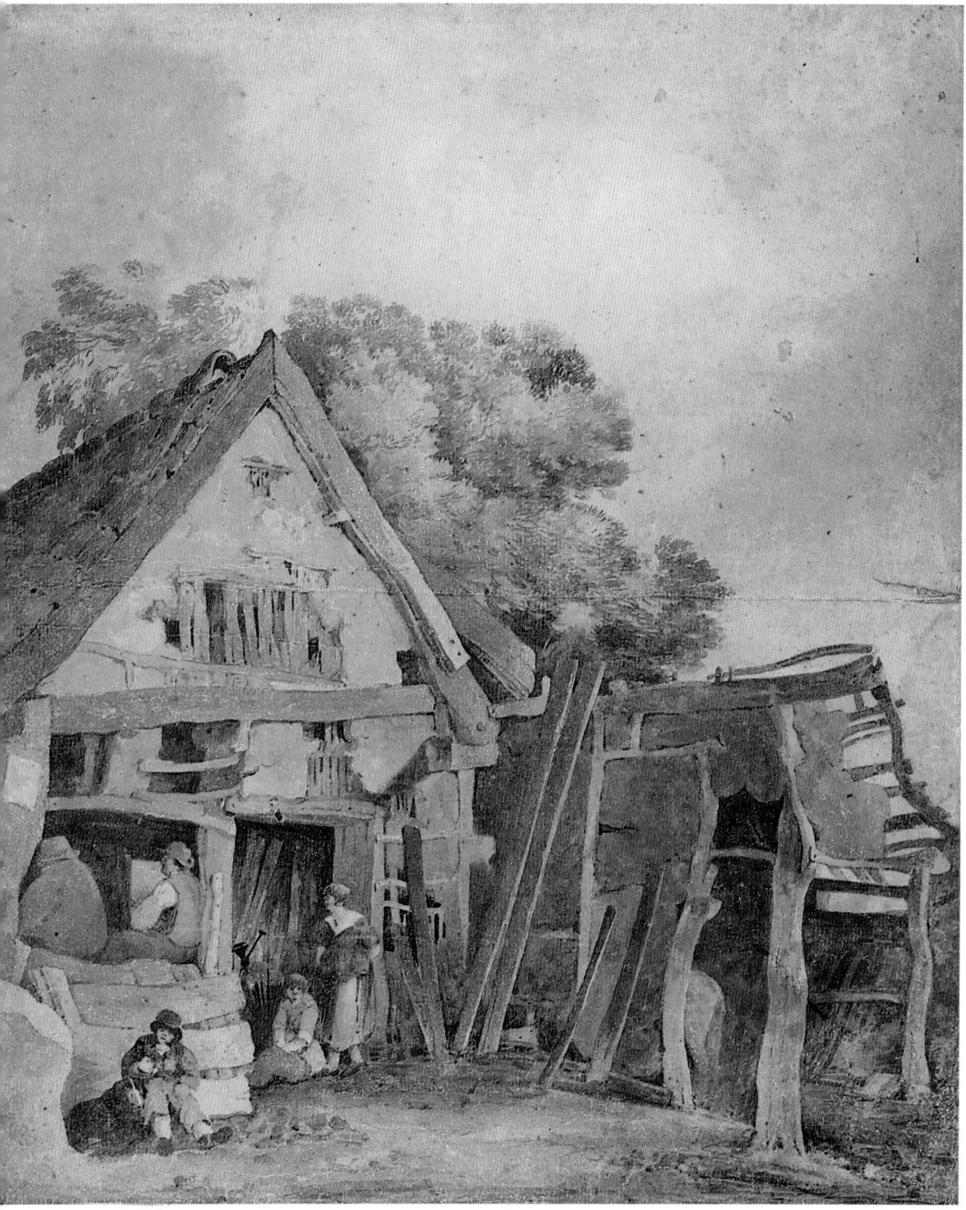

The Blacksmith's Shop, Hingham, Norfolk
John Crome c.1807-11 (watercolour and pencil)

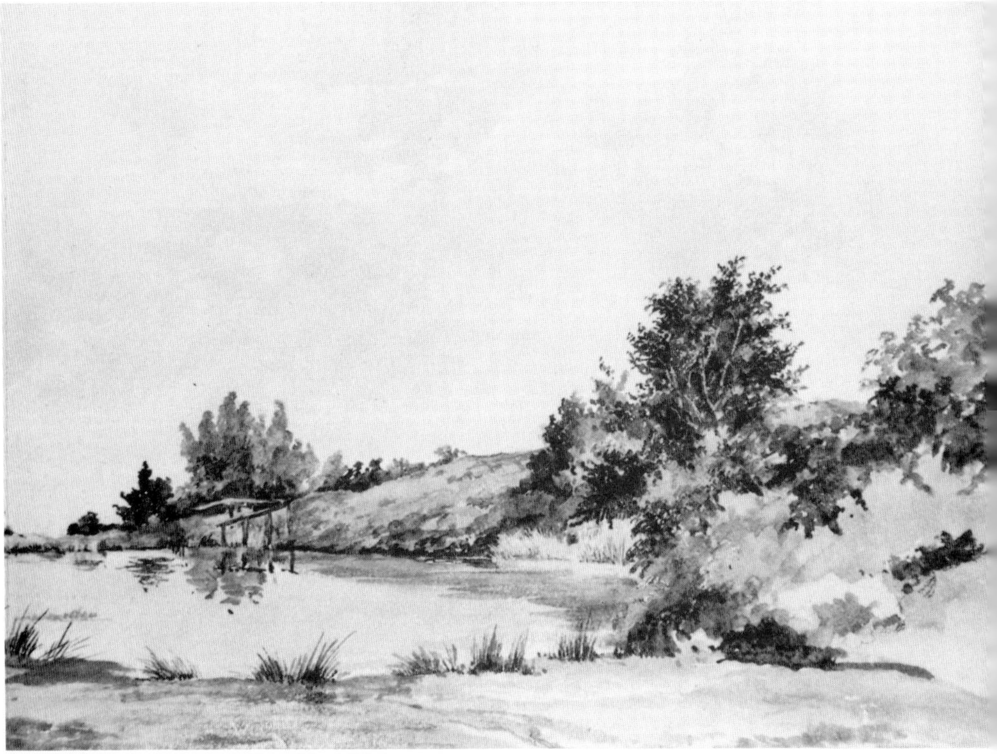

Keston Pond
James Stark
(pencil and watercolour c.1830)

Academy Schools in 1817 where he made friends with William Collins who, in his turn, had known Linnell and Constable. It is fair to say that, to a certain extent, all these painters had some influence on the work of James Stark.

Stark started exhibiting in London in 1811 and enjoyed some considerable success before his return to Norwich in 1819. Working mainly in oils, his work owed much to the influence of Hobbema and Ruisdael as well as Crome and Constable, but his watercolours had a much freer approach and often a simplicity that contrasted sharply with his highly finished, finely detailed oils. Some of his sketches with watercolour and chalk have a spontaneity and sincerity that somehow seems lacking in the oils and one feels that he probably regarded his perfectionist canvases as his livelihood while his watercolour sketches were executed for pure pleasure. It has been suggested that the watercolours represent the fusion of the influence of Crome and Cotman, that the freer watercolours of Cotman exercised a fascination for him and he sought to emulate the technique. It would be difficult to pinpoint any direct influence, though – even if Cotman was the inspiration, Stark's watercolours are as different as the characters of the two men. A number of Stark's watercolours are in the British Museum collection and provide an interesting study of a more enigmatic personality than first emerges from his work.

Another pupil of Crome's, George Vincent, produced some interesting watercolours although, again, he was primarily an oil painter as were the younger Cromes, John Berney Ladbroke and the Stannards who all regarded watercolours as subsidiary to their oils. Nevertheless all of these artists produced watercolours at some time,

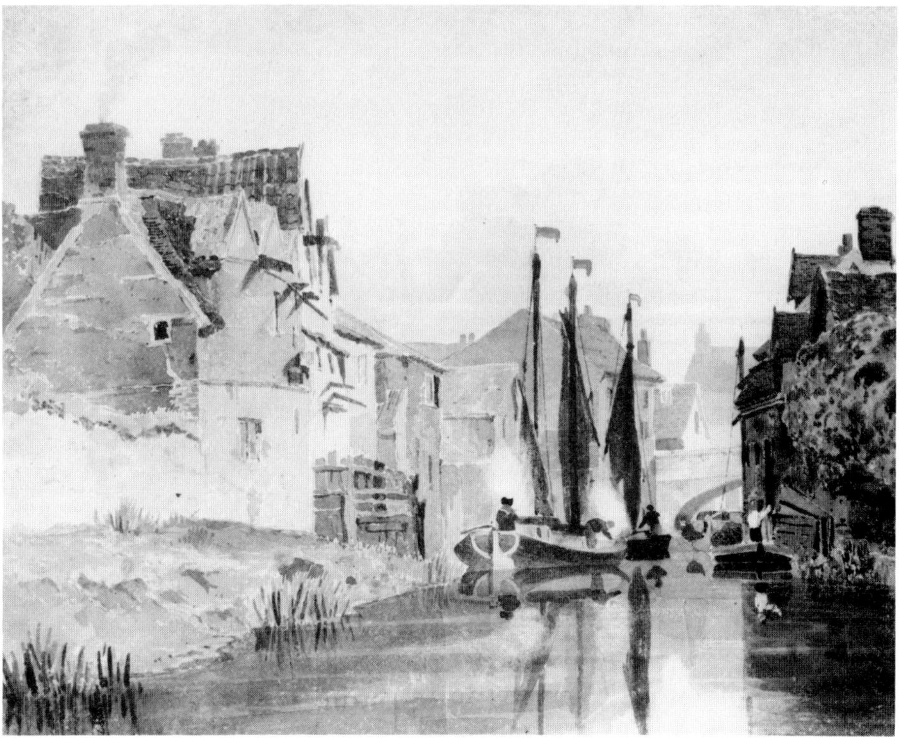

St. James Fyebridge and Whitefriars, Norwich
Henry Ninham (watercolour c.1830)

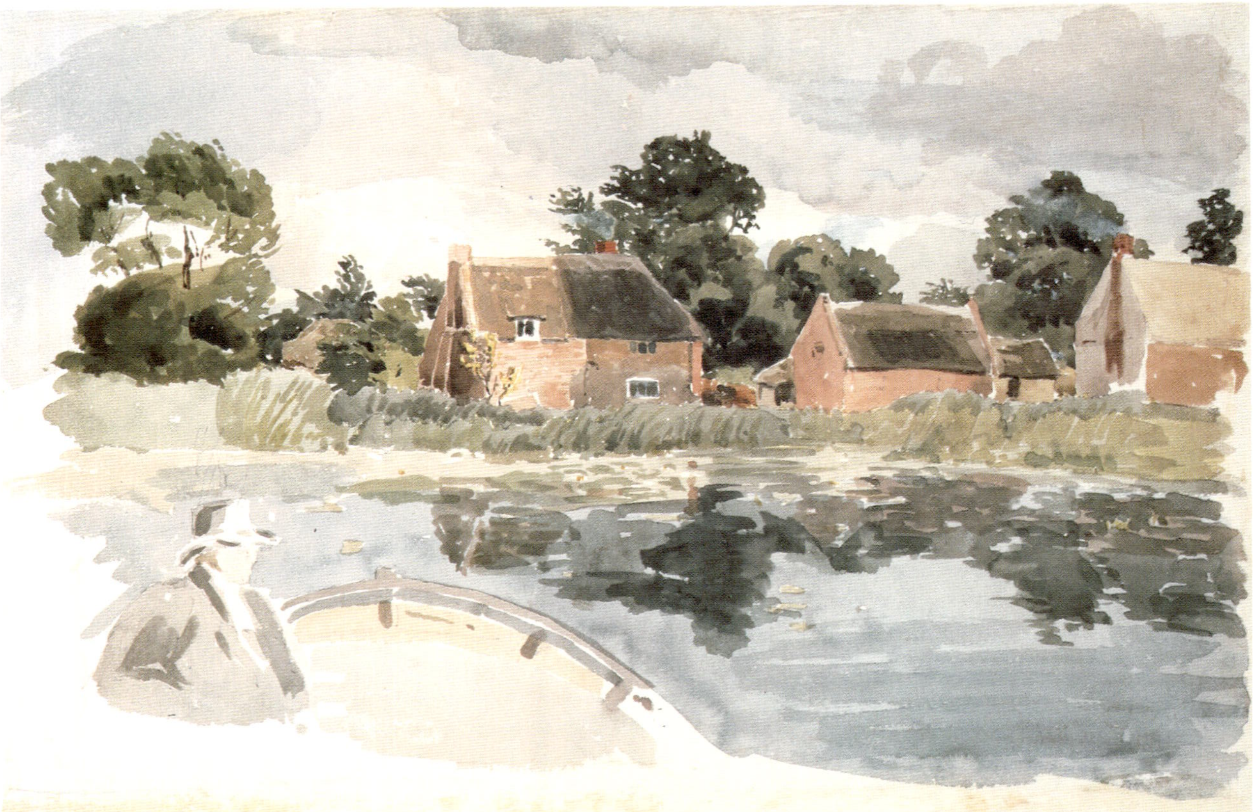

Hoveton Little Broad
John Thirtle (watercolour c.1815)

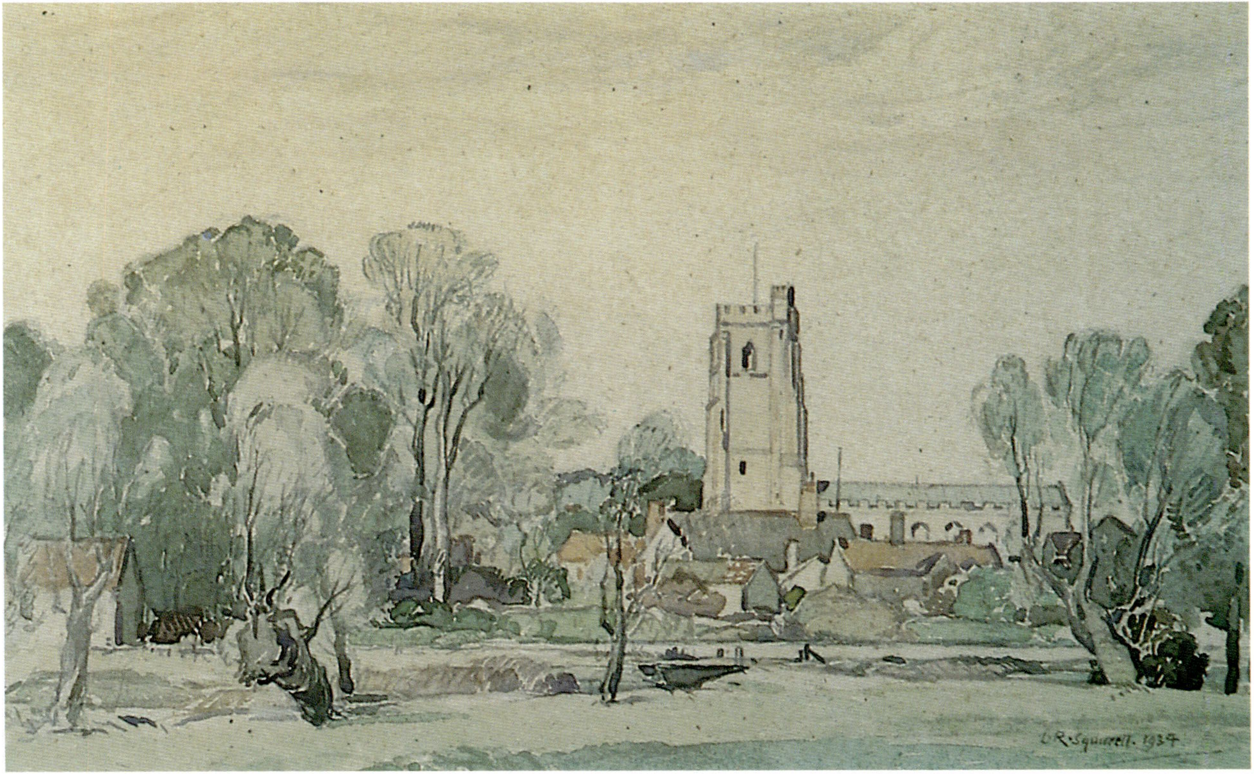

Mildenhall Church from the Meadows
Leonard Squirrell (watercolour 1934)

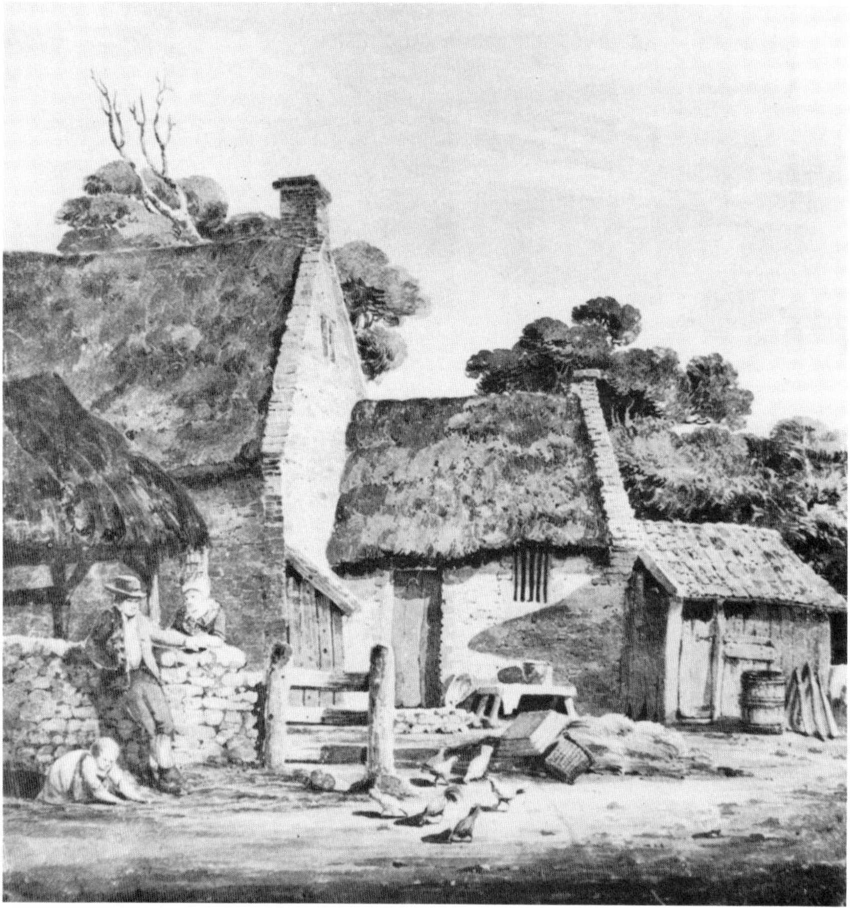

Farmyard Scen
Robert Dixon
(pencil and watercolour c.1809)

many being excellent examples of the medium but, regretably I feel, oils have dominated the early Norwich scene.

One of the earlier Norwich School painters who must not, however, be forgotten in this respect is, of course, Robert Dixon (1780-1815) who was undoubtedly influenced by John Sell Cotman. Drawing was an exceptionally strong point with Dixon which naturally helped his relatively few but extremely competent watercolours. These were executed rather in the late 18th century idiom until in later life he developed a much freer style using simple but very controlled washes. Henry Ninham (1795-1874) is another interesting painter whose quality of drawing earned him the appreciation of John Sell Cotman. His skill as a draughtsman and interest in architectural subjects gave his watercolours a very personal character enhanced by a subtly muted colour palette.

It was really with the second era as it were of the Norwich School painters that more watercolourists of note came on the scene. Thomas Lound (1802-1861) and Samuel David Colkett (1800-1863) are obvious examples although more of Colkett's generally known work is oil. Colkett was a pupil of James Stark which shows in his work although the main influence on his watercolours would seem to be David Cox. Thomas Lound was taught by John Sell Cotman and was essentially a watercolour painter. He too came under the influence of Cox to a degree and there are suggestions of both Crome and Thirtle

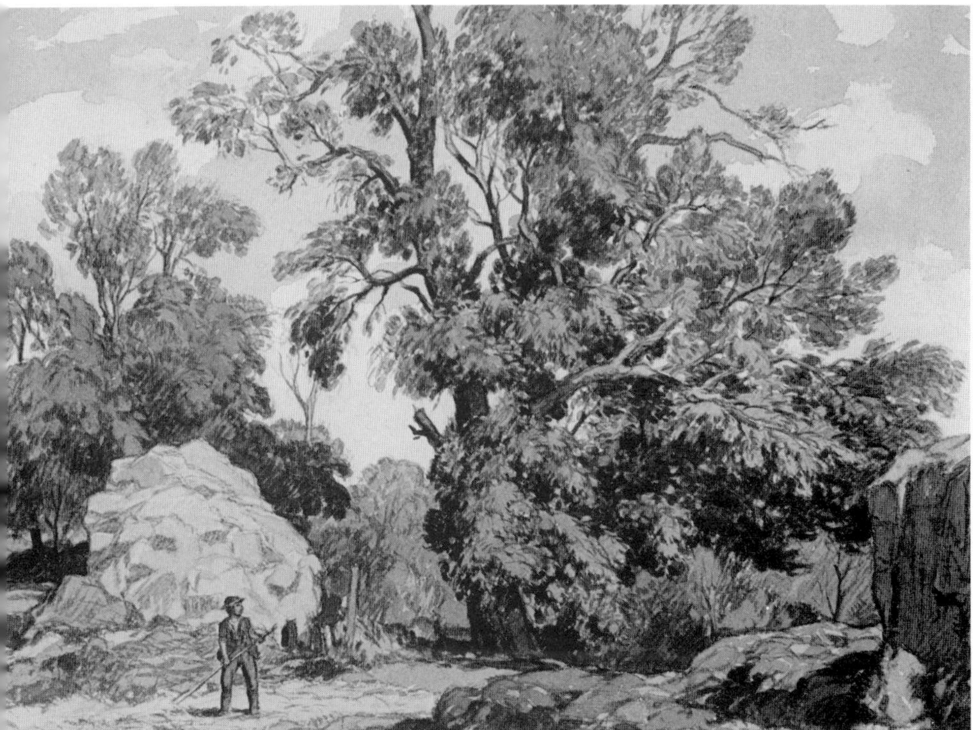

An Old Tree at Tuddenham
Leonard Squirrell (pencil and watercolour 1974)

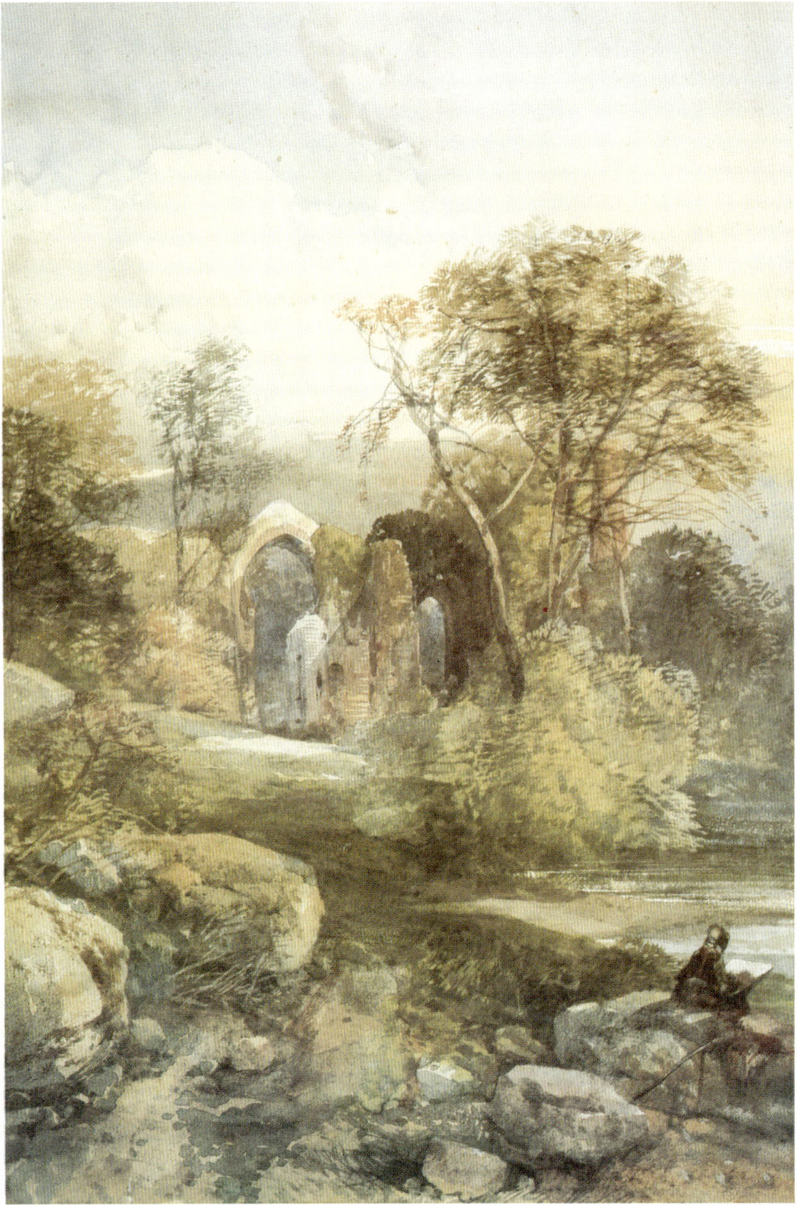

Devon
John Middleton (watercolour)

in some of his work. Maybe these are accidental or coincidental or maybe the inevitable, perhaps unconscious, result of a number of able painters working, teaching and exhibiting together.

There is no doubt that Lound was a highly skilled exponent of the watercolour medium. His work has a fresh, spontaneous quality with beautifully clean washes and his exceptionally keen observation of nature enabled him to add the sort of unexpected detail that hallmarked his work. Lound was not a poor man and his opportunity for reading, collecting and painting without the stress of earning a living undoubtedly added to the quality of his work at its best, although the temptation to experiment and diversify meant that not all his work reached the standard of which he was capable.

Contemporary with Lound and also a pupil of John Sell Cotman was Robert Leman (1799-1863), a watercolourist who has been undeservedly neglected. While obviously influenced by John Sell, he had his own very personal style with, once again, meticulous drawing as its foundation. His pencil drawings are particularly competent and his handling of watercolour in conjunction with this carefully controlled draughtsmanship has a classical quality, probably second only to Cotman,* enhanced by his frequent use of clear light blues and purples. Denis Thomas has written of him,

> 'Leman's drawings are handsome, intelligent and disciplined – a description that applies equally to his watercolours, with their serene washes, restricted range of tones, deft simplification of detail and pale cerulean light.' He also points out his 'reflective, personal response to the landscape, as opposed to the merely picturesque, which seperates the exceptional artist from the rest.'

Clifford comments that 'there is little that is amateurish about much of Leman's work, which would rank high in any company,' and that he was, perhaps, the only one of Cotman's followers to have seized on the classic quality of his work but in his own very distinctive style,

* From time to time Cotman indulged in a classical phase, for instance c.1832-33 when he produced a number of classical landscapes in pencil and watercolour, probably inspired by Bourdon and Poussin whose work always interested him. Classical architecture obviously took its place with other architectural features in his drawings and etchings although in the latter he would sometimes introduce a classical effect in subjects not strictly classical in themselves, on his own admission, for the Piranesi effect.

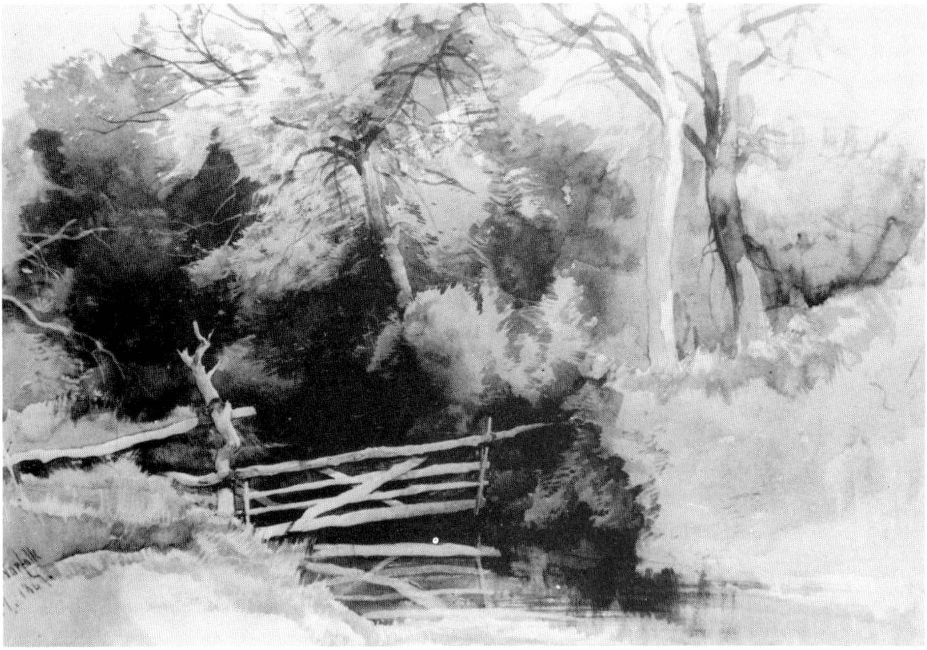

Aldby, Norwich
John Middleton (watercolour c.1850)

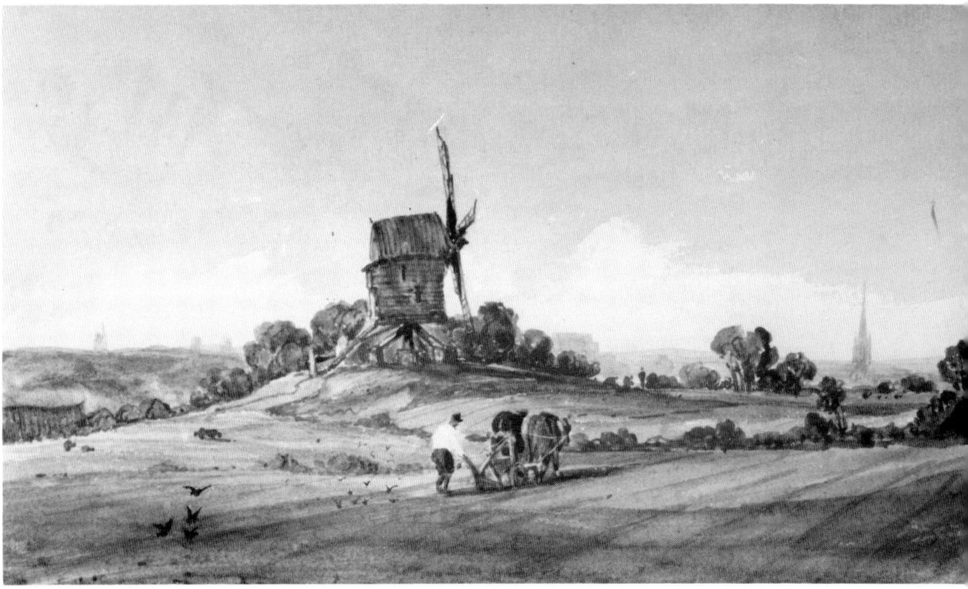

View of Norwich
Thomas Lound (watercolour c.1840)

'his own consistent development of what he had learned from Cotman.' Leman, like Lound, Bright and Middleton, always regarded himself as an amateur but it must be remembered that the word then had a meaning far removed from what Thomas calls 'its modern implication of well meaning incompetence.'

Between Lound, Leman, Bright and Middleton there is a certain contemporary affinity but Leman skilfully used all that he had learnt from John Cotman while at the same time preserving his own identity.

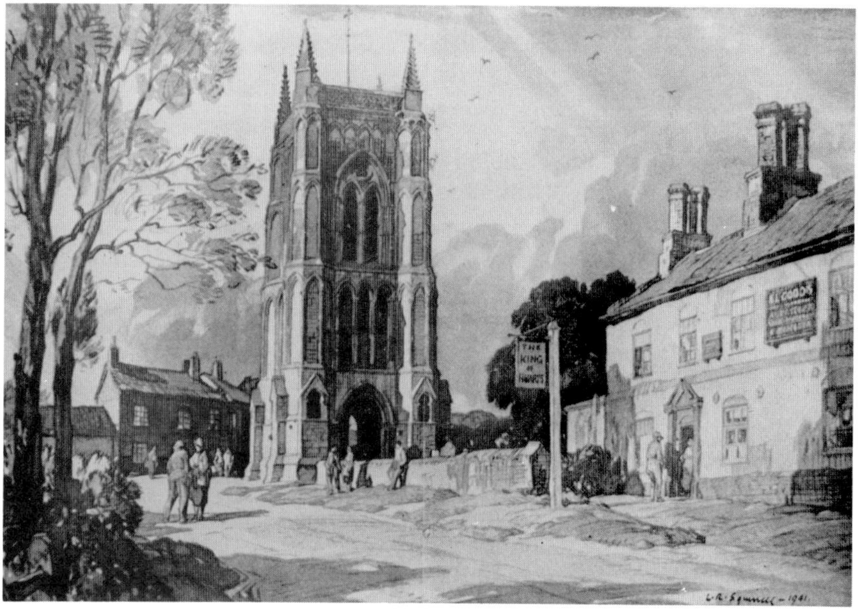

: Tower, West lton, Norfolk onard Squirrell n and wash, 41)

A particularly fine watercolour is 'The Water Gate' which, while displaying the use of certain Cotman teaching, could never be confused with the work of the master; to say this is far from being a disparagement but a compliment to Leman's distinctive style and skill.

By no means neglected has been Henry Bright (1810-1873), the Suffolk artist born in the same year as Miles Edmund Cotman, described by Derek Clifford as 'a star of more than average brilliance.' He studied under John Sell Cotman and John Berney Crome but soon developed his own, very personal, style, often working in mixed media which makes his work difficult to classify. Some of his more innovative work has seemed to belong to a much later artistic era but his draughtsmanship was impeccable whatever the treatment; his pure watercolours were brilliantly executed and, I happen to know, much admired by Leonard Squirrell who was always fascinated by his ingenious use of light. Harold Day writes of Bright, 'Painting and drawing seemed to Henry Bright second nature. His fluency and delicacy of touch are almost unrivalled. He had a great flair for crystalising a subject and accenting salient points in such a way that the viewer is carried into the picture, the eye compulsorily following the beautiful flowing lines.'

Bright was a popular artist in his own time and his income from painting and teaching was well in excess of that of his peers. His very originality coupled with technical competence attracted a large and influential following, also some extremely important and wealthy patrons including the Duke of Wellington and Queen Victoria herself. As well as his talent for the painting itself and his fluency in all media, Bright's actual compositions have an immediate attraction. He had an extraordinary flair for visualising a complete picture before he started to paint and for laying just the right emphasis on the focal points, while the whole of the rest exuded a compelling atmosphere which could be felt as well as seen. One particularly fine piece, 'The Barn', has every possible attribute of a perfectionist watercolour – and a note of Squirrell.

To my mind the supreme tragedy for the Norwich School was the death at only twenty-nine of John Middleton (1827-1856). Had he lived he might well have been one of the most noteworthy artists of the School; thankfully he was a dedicated painter who managed in his short life to produce a significant quantity of outstanding work.

Middleton diversified less than many of the Norwich painters, devoting himself mainly to watercolour as his chosen medium. He handled it brilliantly and one cannot help feeling that his power of observation and appreciation of the beauty of the natural world may have been sharpened by the knowledge that he was so soon to 'look thy last on all things lovely . . .'

Middleton studied under John Berney Ladbroke and Joseph Stannard and was to a degree influenced by his friends and seniors, Henry Bright and Thomas Lound. Lush green growth with sunlight filtering through the leaves and trees, rocks and stones, leafy lanes and old derelict barns provided his favourite subjects, subjects that he handled

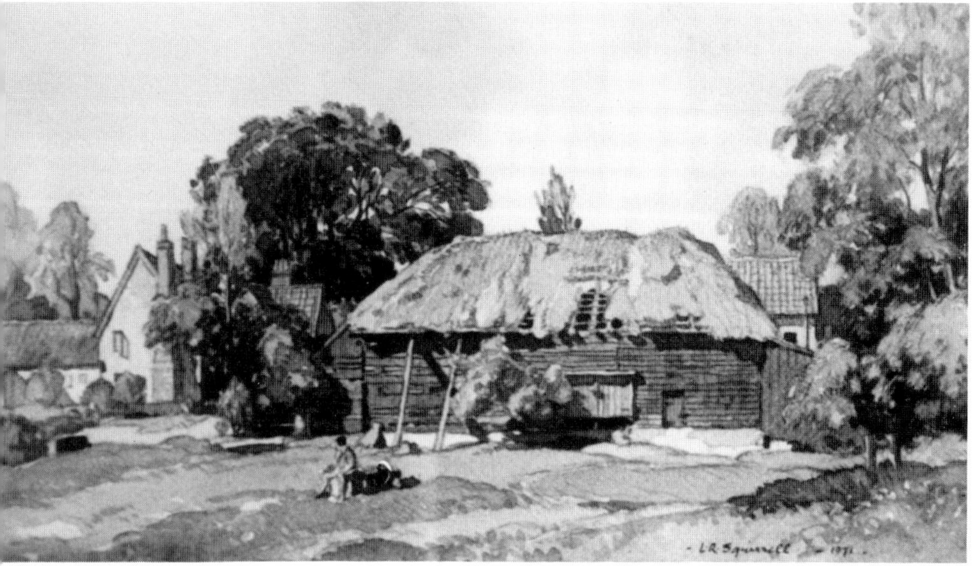

Barn at Tuddenham
Leonard Squirrell (watercolour 1971)

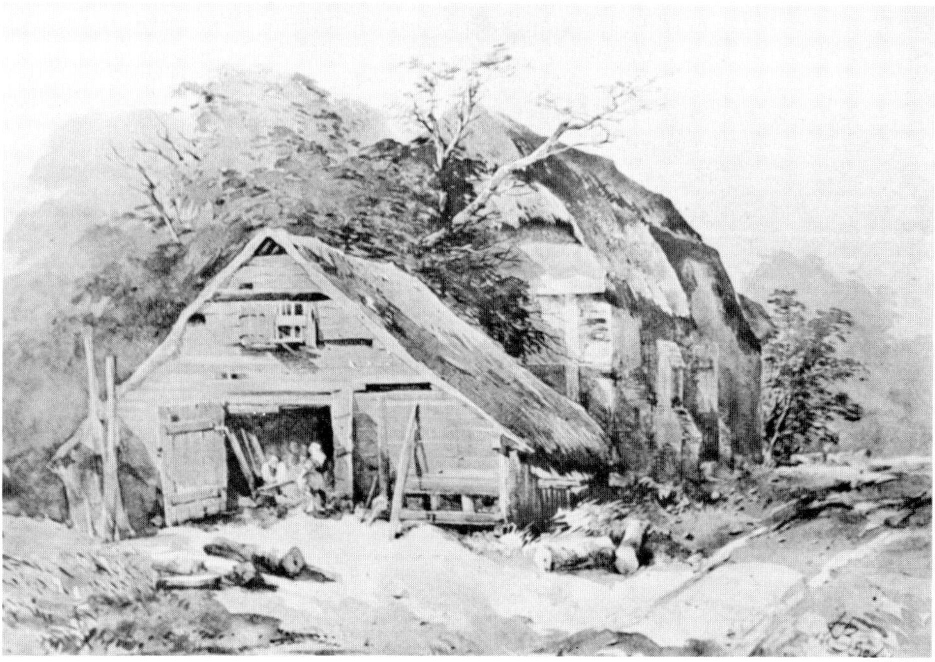

A Barn
Henry Bright (watercolour 1847)

with much more than average skill. His use of light is at times quite breathtaking so much is one made to feel drawn into the warm leafy loveliness he portrays. Derek Clifford says of one of my own favourite works, 'Alby, Norfolk', '. . . we are (more) directly involved in the emotion of the scene, the receding backwater, the sunlight and the shadow, the reflections on the still surface; we can hear the water voles moving under the bank, and the insects humming about the hot foliage, and somewhere behind us in the meadow cattle are pulling noisily at lush grass. It is easy to forget that we are looking at a picture, because it has caught us up so completely in its world of summer sunshine.'

John Middleton's work has a refreshing freedom and in many ways identifies with the best of 20th century watercolours, a combination of good drawing with relaxed but confident painting. Thankfully he was not a poor man and, in his few short years, was in a position to indulge himself in painting without the need to earn a living. His mother is said to have been an able flower painter, probably it was from her that he took his feeling for plants leaves and foliage. We can only speculate on what works of genius he might have produced in a normal lifetime.

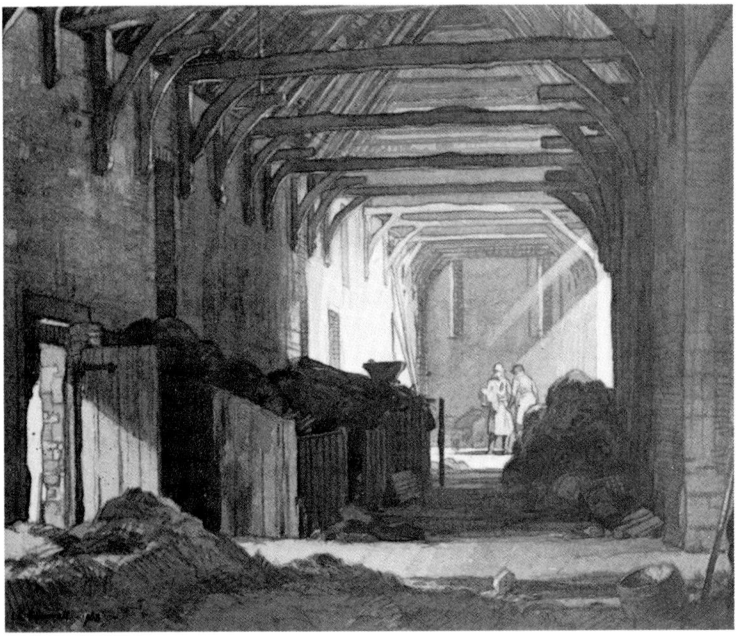

The Paston Bar
Norfolk
Leonard Squirr
(watercolour
1968)

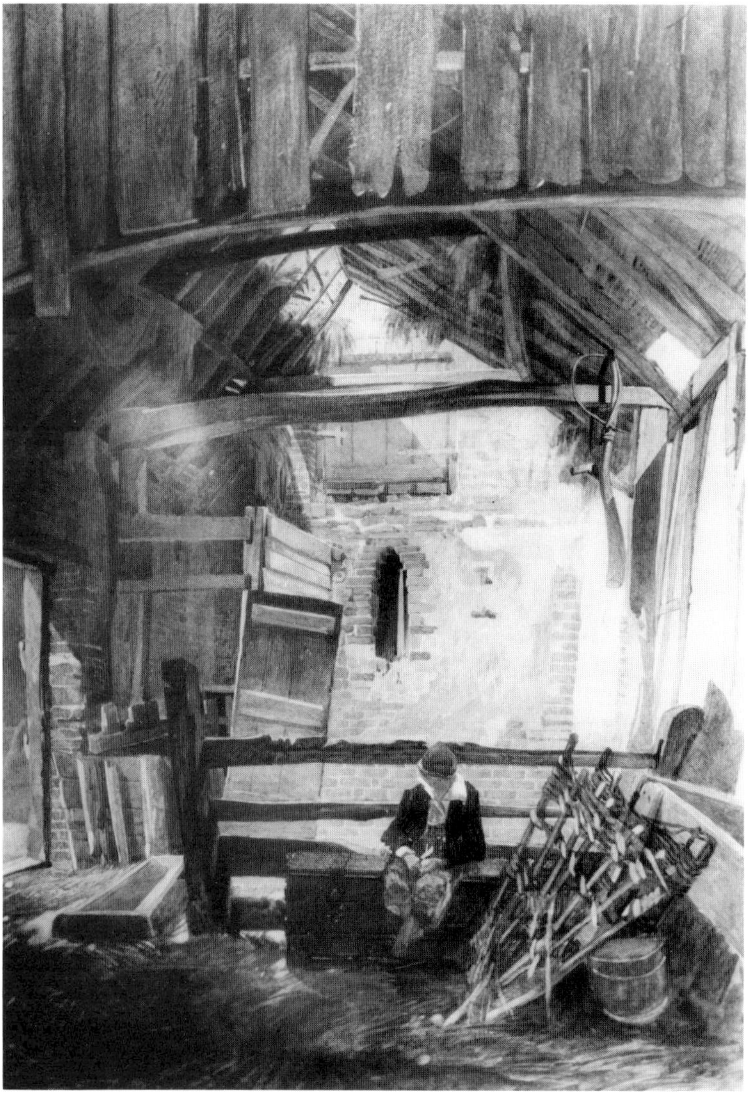

nterior of a Barn
Miles Edmund
Cotman
(watercolour
.1830)

Although for the moment we are passing over John Sell Cotman, it must not be forgotten that the younger Cotmans, Miles Edmund (1810-1858) and John Joseph (1814-1878), produced some excellent work. Miles Edmund Cotman was very much his father's son and they are known frequently to have worked on the same painting. He first exhibited with the Norwich Society at the age of thirteen and, in 1836, was appointed a teacher of Art at King's College to assist his father. He was also an industrious and extremely talented painter and it is sad that the shadow of his father prevented these talents from being fully recognised and appreciated.

Miles Edmund Cotman painted in both oil and watercolour and it is interesting to note that his extremely accomplished watercolours are more detailed than most of those of his father and also more tonally balanced. One might be forgiven for assuming him to be the older painter, in any event their work was frequently confused and, to this day, there are occasional problems of identification. A particular favourite Miles Edmund of mine is 'Interior of a Barn' (Norwich Castle Museum) which is extremely reminiscent of Leonard Squirrell although I never heard the latter mention the sons of John Sell Cotman.

John Joseph Cotman was quite a different matter. Like his father and brother, he was extremely talented but much more erratic than his brother in both his work and personality. Primarily a watercolourist, his work was much more freely painted, more emotional than his brother's, and his colour on occasion could be quite wild. His handling of blues which predominated much of his work is exciting but, in some instances, almost overpowering. At best, though, his work has a very special quality all of its own. Undoubtedly the erraticism was occasioned by his mercurial temperament and periodic mental instability coupled with an addiction to bouts of heavy drinking which impoverished him and ruined his health. Sadly he died in Norwich in complete destitution.

It will be seen that, while there is tremendous variation in the watercolours of the Norwich School, they come together quite naturally and with the feeling of true compatibility so characteristic of the School. In the same way, Leonard Squirrell's work shares this compatibility, the unconscious bond which, of twentieth century artists, belongs to him alone. There have been many excellent East Anglian artists this century, some who have gained greater prestige and predominance than the retiring Squirrell, but not one other can be said to share this intangible sense of belonging with the Norwich painters, a totally natural and unintentional compatibility for Squirrell was, above all things, true to himself.

Chapter 3

THE COMMON DENOMINATOR

I have made a point of emphasising the importance of good drawing as the foundation for whatever medium is subsequently used, a point Leonard Squirrell also firmly impressed on all his students and anyone else who cared to listen. Generally speaking, the Norwich painters were excellent draughtsmen, some quite exceptional, which shows throughout their work. Many of them enjoyed drawing for its own sake and pencil as a medium in its own right, and the craft of etching, where good drawing is absolutely imperative, was practiced by quite a number of them.

Leonard Squirrell was a superlative etcher and engraver and his output in this most exacting of all media, was prodigious. He exploited the medium to a far greater extent than most of the Norwich School etchers who rarely ventured into the realms of mezzotints and aquatints. In 1923 Squirrell was awarded the Silver Medal at the International Printmakers Exhibition, Los Angeles, California, for the mezzotint, 'The High Mill, Needham Market,' in 1925 the Gold Medal for an aquatint, 'Nôtre Dame, Paris', and in 1930 again the Gold Medal for the aquatint 'The Shadowed Corner, Marseilles.' Exquisite pieces as these are, I would rate even higher the aquatint 'Framlingham Castle by Moonlight' and the delightful, tiny mezzotint 'The Wind in the Willows,' a difficult subject handled with exemplary expertise.

Again omitting the Master, John Sell Cotman, let us consider some of the Norwich artists whose drawings and etchings constitute an important dimension of their work.

Some of John Crome's pencil drawings survive but they are unspectacular albeit unfailingly 'correct,' probably sketches for later paintings, for example a drawing in the British Museum, 'View from the King's Head Gardens at Thorpe,' 1806, was the sketch for a painting now in Norwich Castle Museum. Some of his monochrome drawings with pencil and wash or with brush alone are in a different class altogether, in fact Derek Clifford says of these drawings, 'their combination of strength and fragility makes them seem like delicate fragments from an early Chinese scroll painting.'

Crome was also one of the pioneers in the revival of original etching

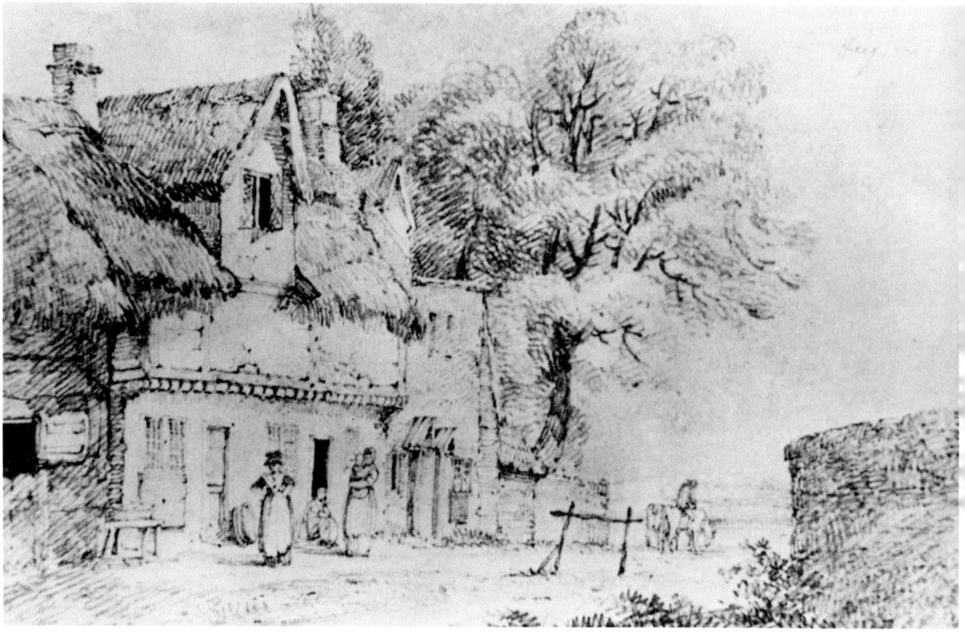

View at Heigha[m]
Norfolk
Robert Dixon
(pencil 1809)

which later became quite popular. He produced quite a number, mainly soft ground, of which about thirty survive. Soft ground etching is a simpler and less involved technique than hard ground and the effect is softer, rather like a pencil drawing as typified in Crome's 'At Bixley' in the British Museum.

Robert Dixon also worked on soft ground etchings about the same time as Crome, concentrating primarily on a series of Picturesque Scenery of Norfolk, thirty eight plates of soft ground etchings. A number of Dixon's surviving pencil drawings and sketches and the basic drawing behind such watercolours as 'St. Leonard's Priory, Norwich,' 1809, show him to be a more imaginative draughtsman than Crome and that possibly the influence of Cotman had given him the assurance and inspiration he needed. 'View at Heigham, Norfolk,' 1809, has almost the quality of a Cotman drawing, so accomplished with the pencil had he become.

Joseph Stannard was an accomplished etcher too, although this seems not generally to be known. His oils were of such fine quality that they tended to obscure the rarer etched work. There are eleven known etchings of very high calibre including a few drypoints; as with his oil paintings and chalk drawings, Stannard was always attracted by

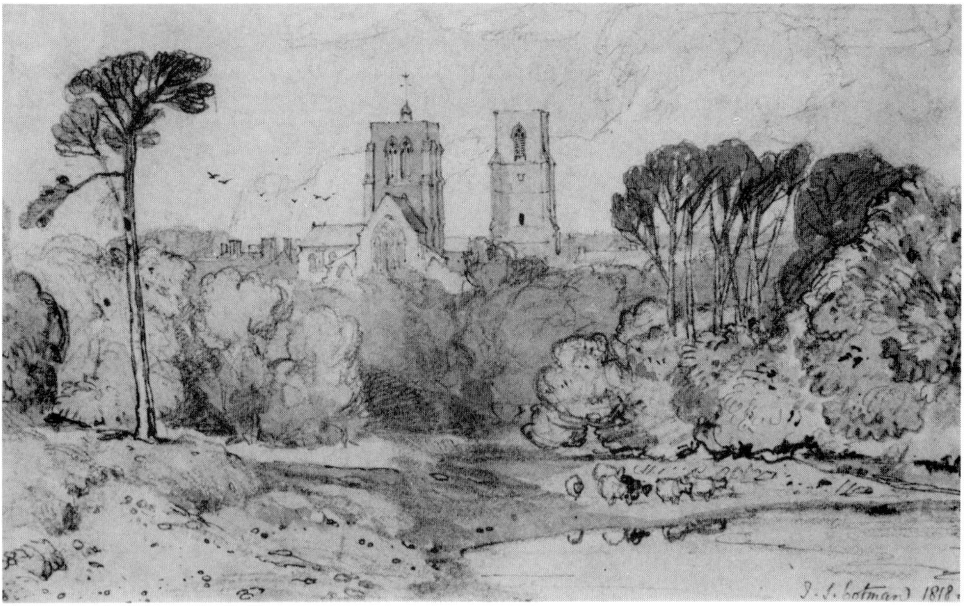

st Dereham,
rfolk
hn Sell Cotman
ncil 1818)

marine subjects.

John Berney Crome executed some very fine drawings in his earlier years but unfortunately these tended to become insignificant as his health deteriorated. There appears to be no record of his ever etching or engraving but James Stark practiced the craft to good effect and a volume of etchings of Norfolk River Views was published in 1834. John Ninham is known for his drawing and engraving, particularly as far as drawings are concerned for those of The Eleven Gates of Norwich. His son Henry was also an able draughtsman and experimented with both drypoint and soft ground etching. He published eight original etchings of Picturesque Antiquities of Norwich, 1842, twenty three views of the Ancient City Gates of Norwich, also Remnants of Antiquity in Norwich and fifteen miscellaneous views of Norwich and Norfolk. David Hodgson as an architectural draughtsman was quite superb even though most of his drawing was expressed in paint. His large oil, 'The Octagon, Ely Cathedral,' is nothing short of a masterpiece of draughtsmanship. In 1843 he completed a series of twenty etchings entitled 'Antiquarian Remains principally confined to Norwich and Norfolk' although these seem almost too influenced by Cotman's drawings.

I have already mentioned Henry Bright whose basic drawing whatever other medium used was quite impeccable; particularly appealing are his little pencil drawings, often on tinted paper and sometimes with a little body colour in crayon or chalk. Very occasionally I have seen this technique practiced by Leonard Squirrell with conspicuous success especially a long narrow drawing of Blackfriars Bridge which I was lucky enough to rescue from an ignominious fate and hand over to a sympathetic restorer. There still exists a number of Bright's pencil and crayon drawings as well as pastels, all of which show a delicacy and sensitivity sometimes lacking in his more innovative oils. But, however innovative, his drawing never falters and it is always particularly beautiful in his studies of old barns, old tree stumps and other natural forms. Bright was never noted for his modesty or slow to use the names of his more illustrious patrons to his own advantage. The Catalogue of the Liverpool Academy in 1836 styles him as 'draughtsman in crayon to Her Royal Highness, the Langravine of Hesse Hamberg!'

The two Cotman sons, Miles Edmund and John Joseph, were as aforesaid and quite naturally bearing in mind their exalted father, excellent draughtsmen and Miles Edmund also produced some interesting etchings ten of which were published by Charles Muskett in 1846. There is also a further, extremely rare, set of eleven etchings. John Joseph's pure drawing was more spontaneous and, to many of us, more satisfying than most of his over flamboyant oils although his watercolours retain a pleasing freshness.

Thomas Lound I have also mentioned previously as a fine draughtsman but it must, of course, be remembered that almost all these people were taught by or by pupils of John Crome or John Sell Cotman, masters of their art. A number of charcoal sketches of Lound's are still with us and from time to time there appears in a saleroom one or more of his distinctive sepia drawings.

Another artist whose drawing is exceptional is John Thirtle who as mentioned in an earlier chapter, used pencil to great effect in his watercolour drawings making it difficult to classify these works – if, indeed, classification is necessary. Small pencil sketches can be found in the corners or margins of many of his watercolour drawings, probably detailed reminders of something he hoped to introduce into the same or later works. Leonard Squirrell used also to do this, here often annotated but, by to-day's standards, these little gems are so 'finished' that they are being removed and framed by collectors as

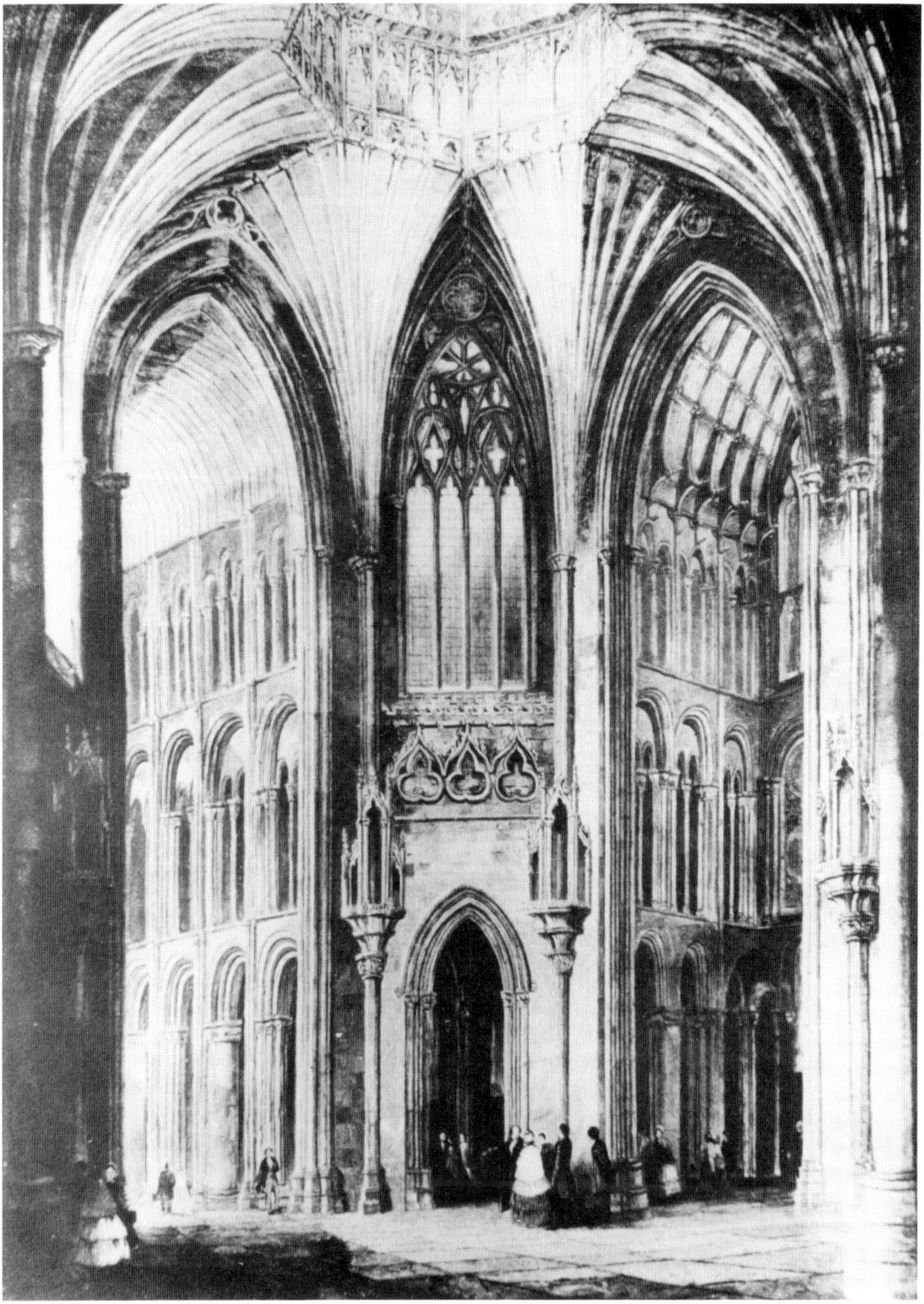

The Octagon, Ely Cathedral
David Hodgson (oil 1858)

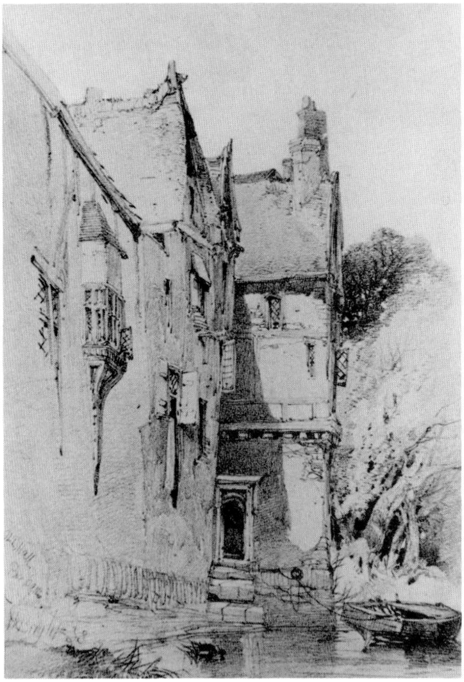

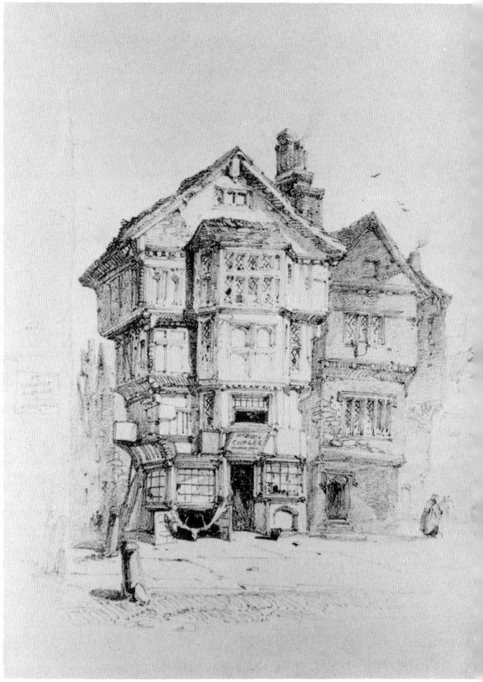

Parham
Drawings by Henry Bright

Saxmundham

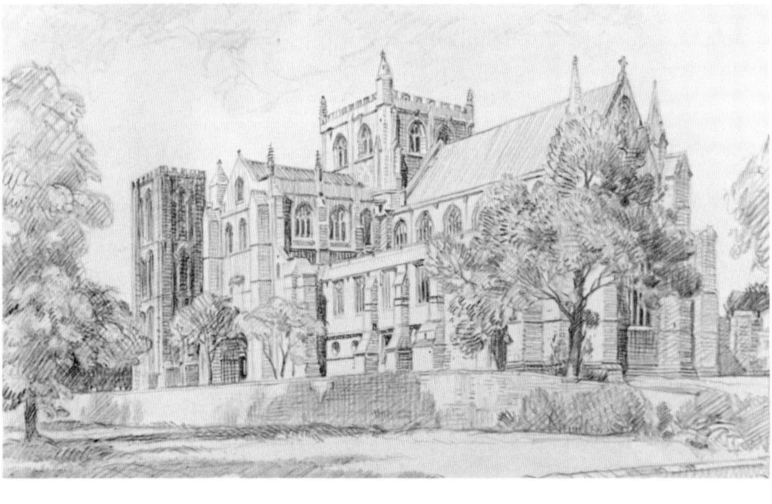

Ripon Cathedral
Leonard Squirrel
(pencil c.1930)

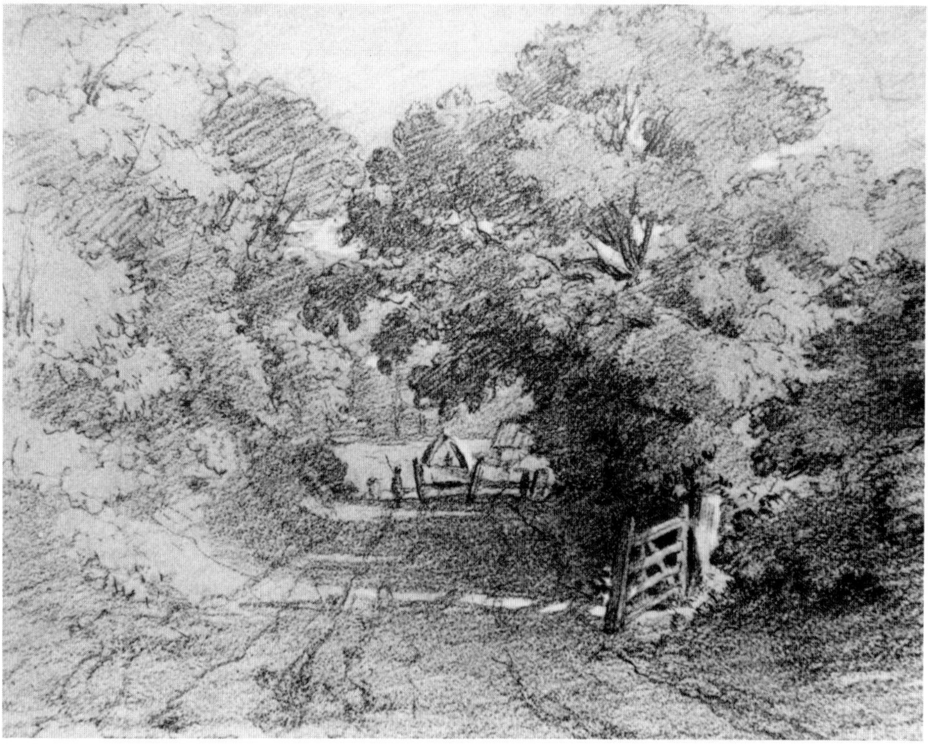

Lane with Covered Cart
Joseph Geldart (chalk, late 1830s)

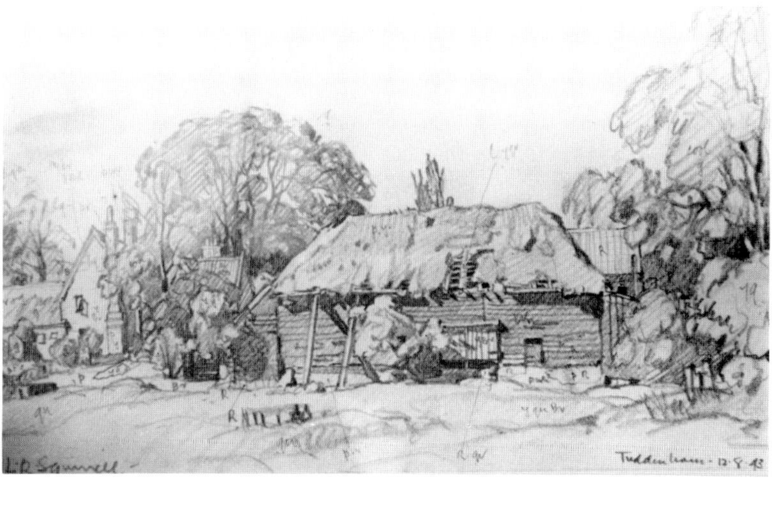

uddenham
eonard Squirrell
encil 1943)

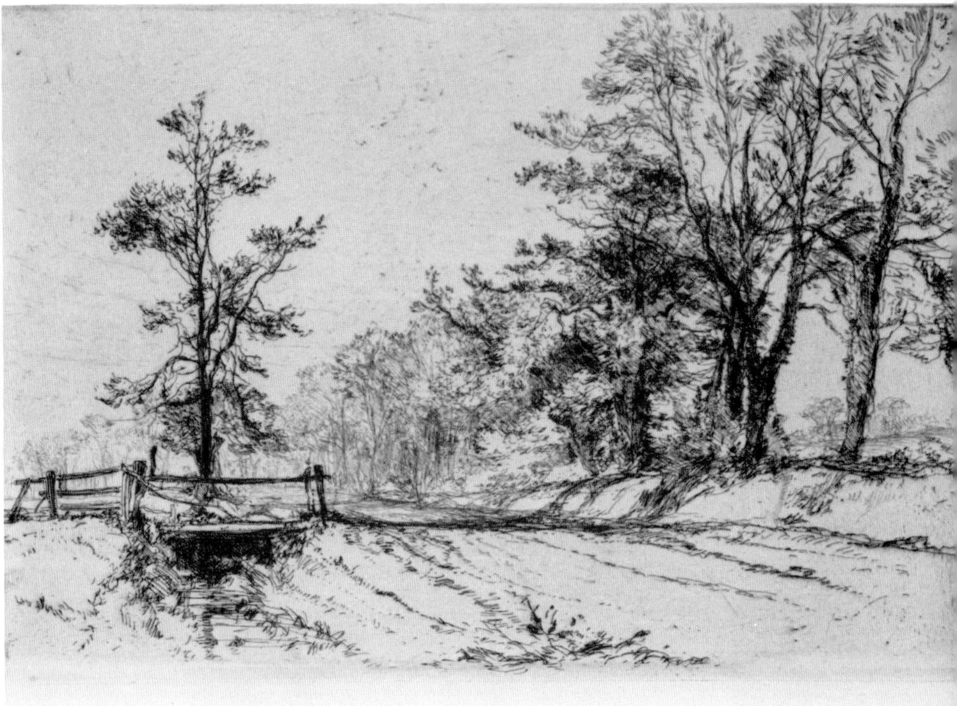

Norfolk Lane
E.T. Daniell
(etching)

small works of art in their own right.

Thirtle's draughtsmanship is illustrated in every watercolour drawing (as opposed to pure watercolour which has been dealt with elsewhere) but his actual pencil drawings indicate even more his consummate talent and skill. Of those I have seen, I find most satisfying 'Bishops Bridge, Norwich' and 'Scene at Gillingham, Norfolk' – each quite different in conception yet both exuding the effortless skill of the true artist/draughtsman. 'Thorpe, 1817,' a more polished drawing perhaps, has exceptional quality and shows some influence of Cotman while remaining unmistakeably Thirtle.

The Rev. E.T. Daniell (1804-1843) is the one artist whose reputation actually rests on his etchings and thereby, of course, his drawings on which etchings are based. Although ordained to the priesthood in 1832, Daniell was always interested in art and was taught drawing by John Crome at Norwich Grammar School. He was also a friend of Joseph Stannard's in whose Norwich studio he spent much time during his vacations from Balliol and from whom he learnt etching. Daniell travelled widely in the eighteen twenties, sketching

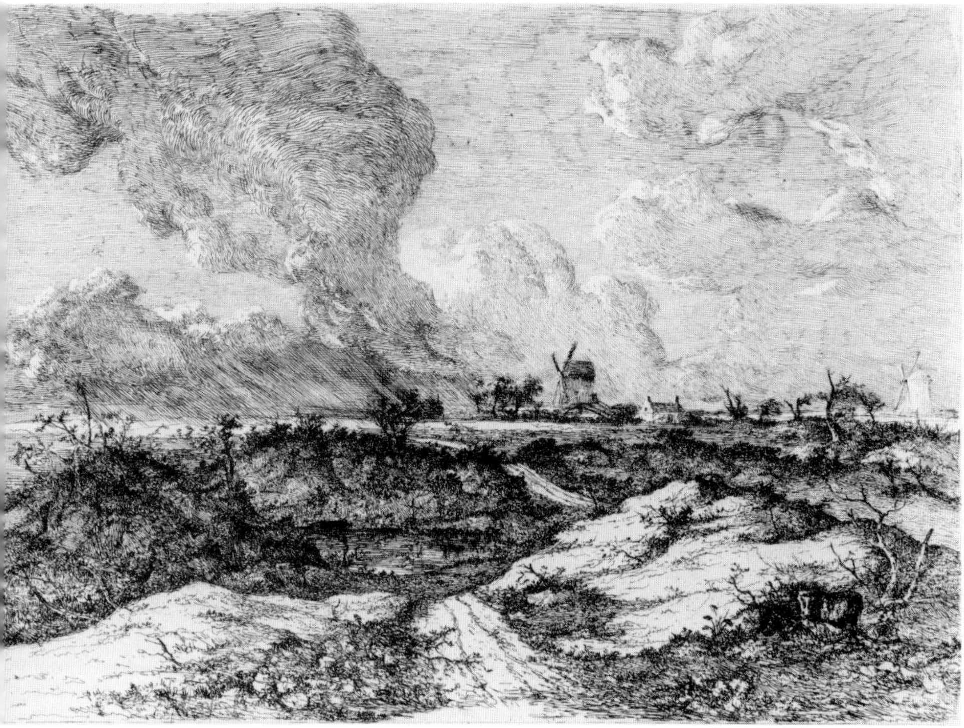

Mousehold Heath, Norwich John Crome (etching c.1810)

and doing a certain amount of watercolour drawing – France, Italy and Switzerland, then back to exhibiting in Norwich in the early thirties.

Although Crome had been his earliest teacher, one rather feels that Daniell took his inspiration from Cotman who, after all, was the greatest draughtsman and etcher. Sadly Daniell's passion for drawing was his undoing; in 1840 he so admired Roberts' Egyptian drawings that he abandoned everything and joined the Lycian Expedition. In Asia Minor he contracted a fever from which he never recovered.

Although in some cases there are only known to be paintings surviving, it would be hard to find a Norwich School painter who did not draw well whatever the medium and this, of course, is one very important area of affinity with Leonard Squirrell to whom good drawing was all important. Of those who have left us particularly fine pencil drawings (with the exception of John Sell Cotman himself) the most important include John Thirtle, Henry Bright, Robert Dixon and Robert Leman. Most of Leman's known work is in watercolour or pencil, his pencil drawings being particularly sensitive; as Derek

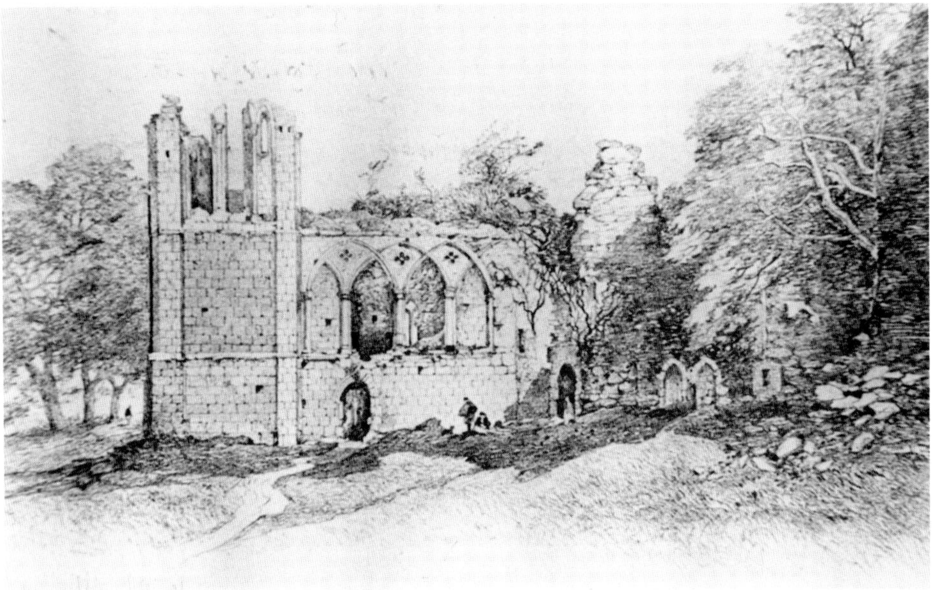

Easby Abbey, Yorkshire
Robert Leman (pencil 1861)

Clifford asserts, his were faultless pencil drawings of even level of professional brilliance, adding 'their fault lies in their faultlessness.' Undoubtedly Leman was influenced by Cotman as indicated by such drawings as his 'Easby Abbey' and he is also known to have copied Cotman's drawings, possibly as exercises. His admiration for John Sell is born out by his collection of over two hundred Cotman drawings and watercolours and proof copies of nearly all his etchings which were sold on Leman's death.

Although Robert Ladbroke's teaching is not rated as highly as that of Crome and Cotman, he too insisted on good drawing and this is again reflected in his pupils' work. Joseph Stannard, for instance, was a good draughtsman and as well as his masterly paintings produced some impeccable drawings in chalk and crayon which included some competent figure studies. Ladbroke's own son, Henry, produced some very detailed drawings, usually the basis of paintings, executed with great care and attention. His output was limited but became, for a time, much sought after. John Berney Ladbroke studied under Crome becoming a drawing master himself and eventually taking over some of his father's teaching connections. Although most of his exhibition work was executed in oils, the power of his draughtsmanship is plainly evident.

Another pupil of both John Crome and Robert Ladbroke was Charles Hodgson whose fine architectural drawings earned him the appointment of Architectural Draughtsman to the Duke of Sussex. In whatever medium he worked, his architectural draughtsmanship was nigh faultless. His aforementioned son, David, inherited his father's talent becoming drawing master at Norwich Grammar School and, like his father, he was honoured by H.R.H. the Duke of Sussex to whom he was appointed Painter of Domestic Architecture.

Antony Sandys (1806-1883) has received less attention than many of the Norwich School painters but he, too, was a fine draughtsman and produced a good collection of landscape and portrait drawings, also some interesting studies of birds and plants. Although John Middleton is best known as a watercolourist, in his tragically short life he produced some very beautiful drawings and also a number of etchings including some copper plate. A set of his etchings was published in 1852 and can be seen in the Castle Museum, Norwich. It is said that he went on drawing as long as he had the strength to hold a pencil.

So it will be seen and understood that good draughtsmanship constitutes the rock on which the Norwich School was built. Undoubtedly this foundation of good drawing has been an important factor in holding the Norwich School together and which will go on distinguishing these painters as long as their work shall live. Where else can one find a school of painters working in such a variety of media over such a range of subjects in so many individual styles yet who are all immediately recognisable as being irrevocably involved with each other largely, there is no shadow of doubt, because of the shared ability to produce such faultless, meaningful basic drawing. Is it surprising, then, that Leonard Squirrell, sharing this common bond, is more and more frequently being referred to as 'the last of the Norwich School.'

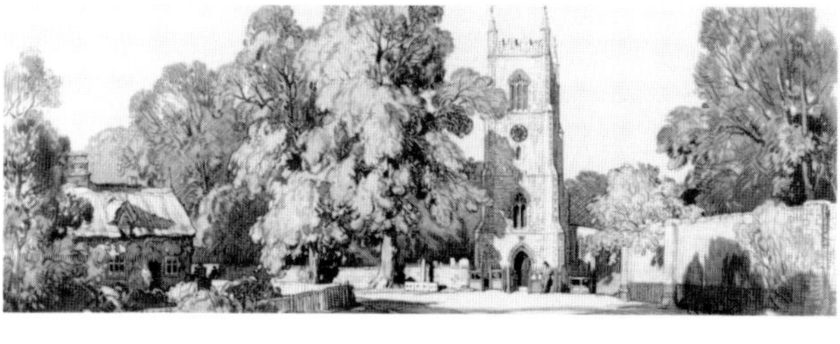

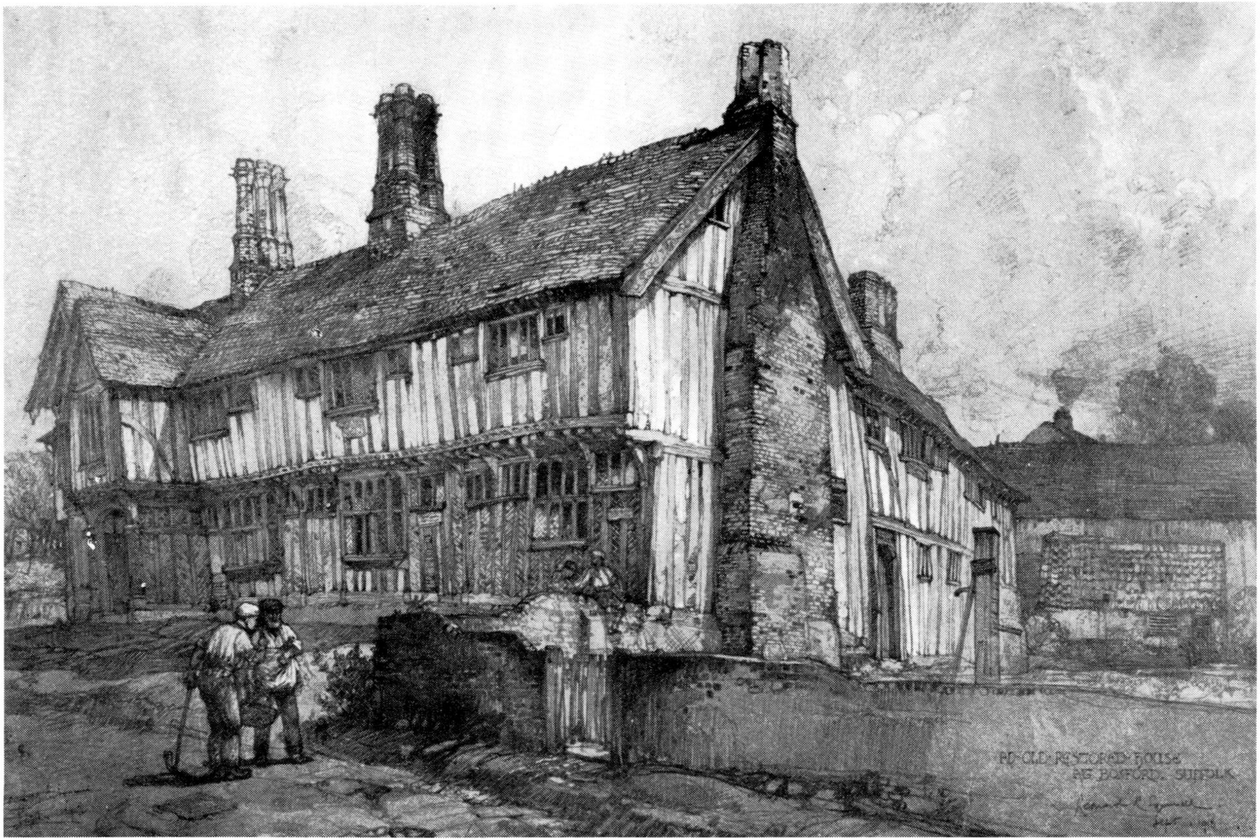

Old Restored House, Near Boxford
Leonard Squirrell (pencil and wash 1913)

Chapter 4

THE COTMAN CONNECTION

'. . .the most perfect examples of pure watercolour ever made in Europe.' Laurence Binyon

Perhaps by relating any painter to the Norwich School to examine the relationship with John Crome or John Sell Cotman is to start, as it were, at the beginning of a dynasty, for the sons and pupils of both gradually handed down their mentor's knowledge and talent, supplemented in each generation by the inspiration of the individual yet, right through the following, embodying something that derived from either or both of the two Masters.

Although interested in the Norwich School as such with a special place for Henry Bright, Leonard Squirrell acknowledged his own particular admiration for and affinity with John Sell Cotman in his book, 'Practice in Watercolour,' wherein he admits to not becoming particularly excited about watercolour 'until we come to Thomas Girtin, J.M.W. Turner and John Sell Cotman.' It is interesting to note that Cotman was himself influenced to a degree by both the other two artists* although his admiration of Turner did not extend to what he referred to as 'his idiosyncratic phase.' Having said that, there is no doubt at all that Turner's unusual colour consciousness and colour co-ordination helped to inspire Cotman's own and to awaken in him an awareness of the importance of colour and light and the juxtaposition of colour as a means of artistic expression. No doubt he would have read Ruskin on Turner – '. . .there is no spot of colour in his work that is not modulated. In the drawings of his earliest phase as in the

* Footnote: Cotman went to London at the age of sixteen, first to Ackermanns where he was mainly colouring aquatints, then to Dr Thomas Monro's 'academy.' Dr. Monro acted as host, tutor and sponsor to a number of promising young artists including Girtin and Turner – although it is likely that they had left his tutelage by the time Cotman joined Dr. Monro, it would have been through him that Cotman met the two older painters as well as his contemporaries, Paul Sandby Munn, Joseph Farrington, Louis Francia and T.R. Underwood.

style that succeeded it, he leaves no broad patches of which one can say 'the whole of that is one colour.' But he does not destroy the breadth in effect of his drawing by this concern with its parts.'

While paying tribute to each of these artists, Squirrell adds, 'I may as well say without any further preliminaries that my greatest stimulus has come from John Sell Cotman. Even before seeing how noticeably his works have gained in reputation in recent years, I felt that in sensitiveness of temperament and in the selective artistry of his handling, he stood out signally from his contemporaries. It may be that his work has appealed to me from some affinity of temperament, and because he belonged to and portrayed my own East Anglia – but there it is. I still marvel at the quality of his art, produced as it was under conditions of discouragement, indifference, and at times acute depression.'

The expression 'affinity of temperament' intrigues me. John Sell Cotman, always temperamentally mercurial, in later life suffered from spells of almost manic depression which could quickly change to a fresh enthusiasm for life and work and a sudden resurrection of charm and energy, while Leonard Squirrell, on the surface at least, was steady, calm and unruffled, always appearing the same – solid and reliable. His daughter, Annette, tells of the terrible period of depression he suffered following the death of her brother, his only son, when for some time he was unable to concentrate on his work or anything else; this surely, though, is the natural and inevitable reaction to such a tragedy and not inborn temperament. Maybe none of us really knew Leonard Squirrell or what was hidden under that sanguine exterior.

It must be emphasised that Leonard Squirrell had no thought of 'copying' Cotman – or anyone else. As W.F. Greeves wrote in 1960, 'Cotman's method of using watercolours certainly influenced Leonard Squirrell, as it has done many another of the best painters in watercolour ever since Cotman's days, but Squirrell has always been essentially himself.' At times to experiment with another artist's technique but bringing to it ones own individuality, style and colour sense is all part of reaching artistic maturity. Cotman and Squirrell were both impeccable draughtsmen and at the level of straightforward drawing are as basically similar as two artists can be who have been rigorously schooled* and relentlessly self-disciplined in that essential common denominator, backed up by a comparable though exceptional talent, that essential but intangible ingredient. Again to quote Greeves,

'The main difference lies in the period rather than the power; it is a certain quaintness which distinguishes the architecture of Cotman's drawing, so greatly enhanced by his superb use of sepia.' Yet again, self-expression comes across, the same subject can be drawn with characteristics peculiar to the individual but still be totally correct while simply being totally correct cannot by any means ensure that the work has the charisma of a Cotman or Squirrell.

In the cases of John Sell Cotman and Leonard Squirrell, a common interest in architectural drawing on the one hand and drawing from nature on the other meant that their subjects could only be similar, even sometimes overlapping, and the frequent necessity of making preliminary sketches for use as later 'finished' drawings, watercolours or etchings meant that at all levels there would be similarity for good drawing is good drawing – the illustrations I have used say it all. Many of the Norwich School artists under Crome or Cotman became comparable draughtsmen to a point, some in their own subjects even equal, but with the introduction of colour be it oil or watercolour, much more of the individual artists' personality came out in self-expression within the traditional limits of the time and not as an excuse for gimmickry as the term is so often used today.

* Footnote: Squirrell probably had the benefit of more formal art education. Ipswich School of Art under George Rushton, R.I., gave excellent basic training and, at eighteen, Squirrell won a Gold Medal for a set of drawings in a National Competition for Schools of Art. He won a British Institute Scholarship to the Slade where he studied under the famous Professor Tonks and Wilson Steer. The formidable Tonks would wring the last ounce of talent from anyone with even a modicum of ability.

Cotman had the benefit of intensive practice in his years of drawing for the printsellers and other similar work, also judging by the eminent artists Dr. Monro turned out, the three years spent with him must have been more than constructive.

It is interesting to note that neither artist is known to have had artistic forbears. At the time of Cotman's birth the assistant to the City midwife was one John Crome who delivered some medicine for the baby to the Cotman home. Young Crome was known to play such pranks as mixing his master's medicines regardless of the patients' ailments. 'Did he,' writes Kitson, 'Puck-like, add a few drops of his own genius to the teething mixture delivered for John Sell Cotman?'

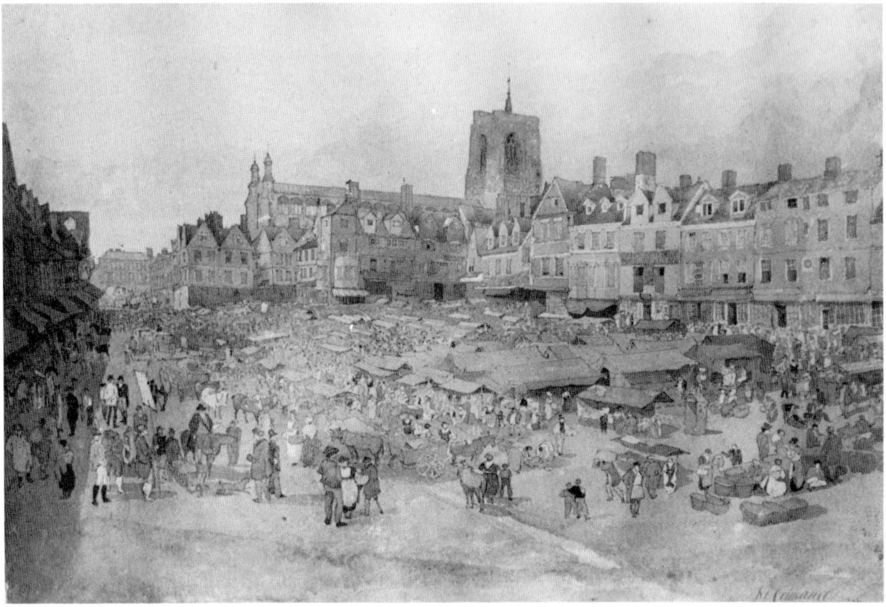

Norwich Market Place
John Sell Cotman (watercolour 1807)

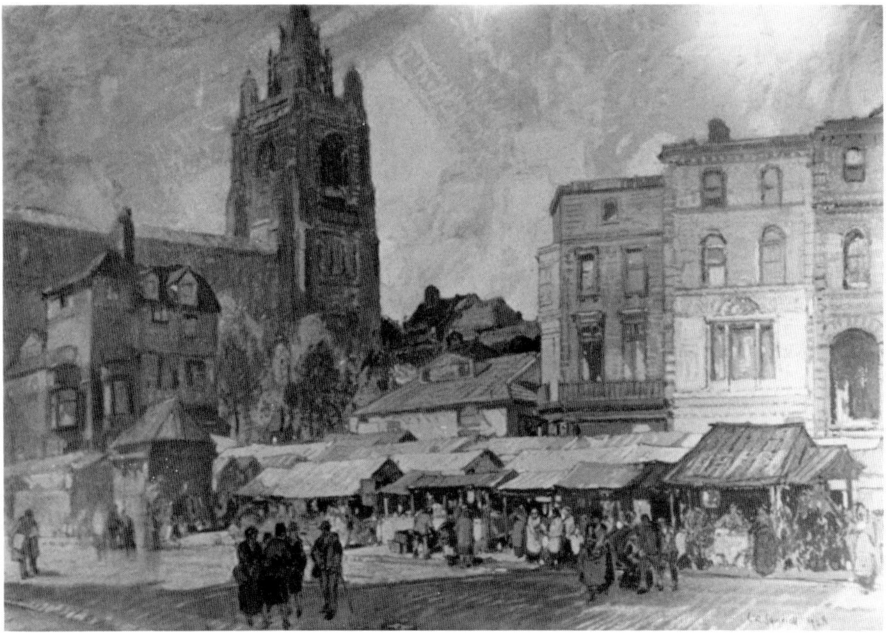

Norwich Market Place
Leonard Squirrell (pastel 1928)

York Minster, from the South East
Leonard Squirrell (pencil and watercolour c.1930)

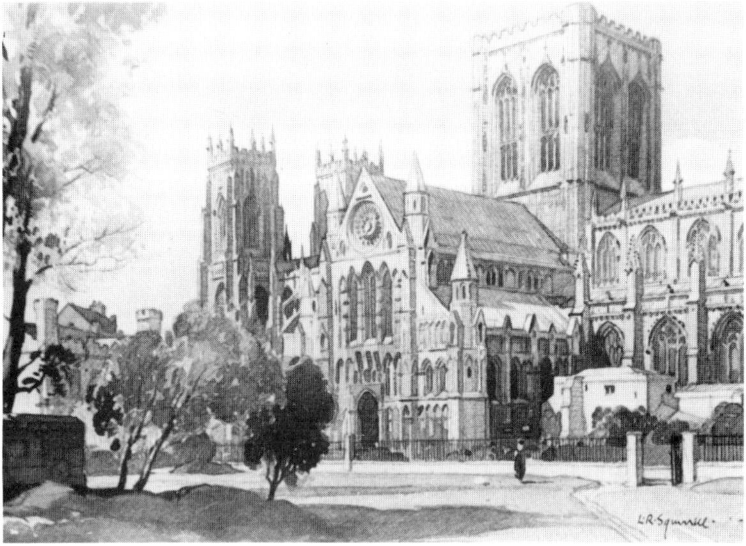

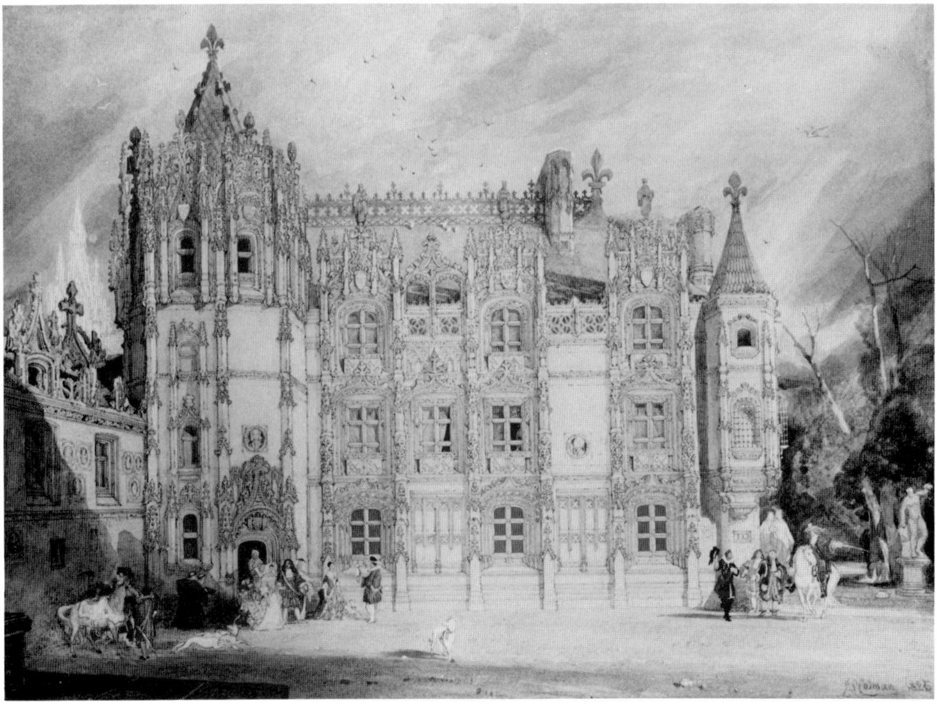

Abbatial House of the Abbey of St. Ouen at Rouen
John Sell Cotman (pencil, ink and watercolour 1825)

It was as a watercolourist that John Sell Cotman most attracted Squirrell – 'Cotman's power of expressing the natural scene in a way which is quite convincing from a representational standpoint, and yet personal and distinctive in the *way* it is expressed, has embodied for me the ideal aim in watercolour.' At the same time, Squirrell was the first to admit that there were times when Cotman's extravagant colouring and more innovative techniques went against the grain. Good drawing was the foundation they both shared and accepted as the absolute essential – no doubt because the quality was so comparable. Cotman's drawing was almost taken for granted by Squirrell, the latter even admitting that certain of Cotman's drawings could be wooden and 'drawing-masterish' which he blamed on the drudgery of teaching. It is actually open to question whether these drawings were necessarily Cotman's own – he produced hundreds and hundreds of drawings for students to copy and occasionally these copies can make identification difficult. But that is by the by.

Squirrell notes that at best Cotman 'reached a pinnacle of watercolour at which he has not been surpassed since his death a hundred years ago,' going on to his comment quoted above about the perfect combination of truth to nature and personal expression. Herein lies both the similarity and the difference in most of the two artists' watercolours – each was an exceptional draughtsman, each had an exceptional vision and ability to put down what he saw, but each had that individual, magical gift of personal expression that turned the work into something only his own. I quote again,

'To depict these essentials (viz. the essential quality or characteristic of a subject) with a discerning and personal artistry, so that one adds a statement of ones own to the actual facts which are seen, is to prove oneself – even if only humbly and gropingly – an artist and not a human camera. But before this conscious variation or 'interpretation' of the natural scene is attempted, the student must have long and patient study of the actuality of things, both to accumulate knowledge by truthful observation, and to perfect the craftsmanship with which to express himself successfully – if he really *has* anything to say.'

Cotman was a much more uneven painter than Squirrell, not necessarily in terms of quality although occasionally that comes into it, but, for instance, in certain of Cotman's more innovative work when he goes so mad with colour that the whole is almost garish. In the main my preference is for his more monochrome watercolour drawings or those in generally lower key although some of the stronger ones such as 'Storm on Yarmouth Beach,' 1831, and 'Stormy Weather,' 1831, have tremendous dramatic appeal.

* * * * * * * * * * * * * * * *

Kitson makes much of the early years of the 19th century as being very important in the development of Cotman's watercolour painting, perhaps starting with his second trip to Yorkshire in the company of Paul Sandby Munn, when the washed drawings took a new turn, the sepia and (regretably fugitive) indigo washes gave way to more colour, pinks, browns and yellows, giving a new warmth and more vibrant personality. Kitson maintains,

'The year 1805 is perhaps the most important one in the whole story of Cotman's artistic development, for it was then that he entered upon his kingdom and produced work of individual distinction. He had advanced step by step in his self-education as an artist. At first he had imitated the drawings of the earlier watercolourists; then at Dr. Monro's house he had been brought into touch with the new outlook and new methods of Turner and Girtin. Afterwards, in working with colleagues at the Drawing Society, he had reached the position of a leader amongst members owing to his livelier imagination and greater technical skill.' He had left his companions behind and, with new confidence and self development, 'was beginning to record the lyrical aspect of Nature.' He was taking much greater care with composition as well as broadening considerably the scope of his subjects.

In his architectural work and landscapes with buildings, Cotman's beautiful drawing remained always in evidence, but those sweeping washes of pure colour, skilfully laid down and backed up by his draughtsman's skill produced some outstanding results; all the time, too, this new found artistic maturity was adding to his confidence and stature. Most compelling of all are the works of what has come to be known as the 'Greta Period', particularly two small studies of the Bridge itself now in the British Museum of which, with others, Kitson writes, 'Both are close studies of trees, seen in the midst of a wood. They are difficult subjects yet Cotman has sifted the haphazard growth and woven his patterns so subtly that the stillness and the fragrance of the scenes can be felt. Another – 'The Scotsman's Stone' – is a drawing of the great boulder which lies in the river bed a couple of miles above Greta Bridge. Here the brown water of the moorland trout stream, as it flows rapidly past the rock, is rendered with an ease and

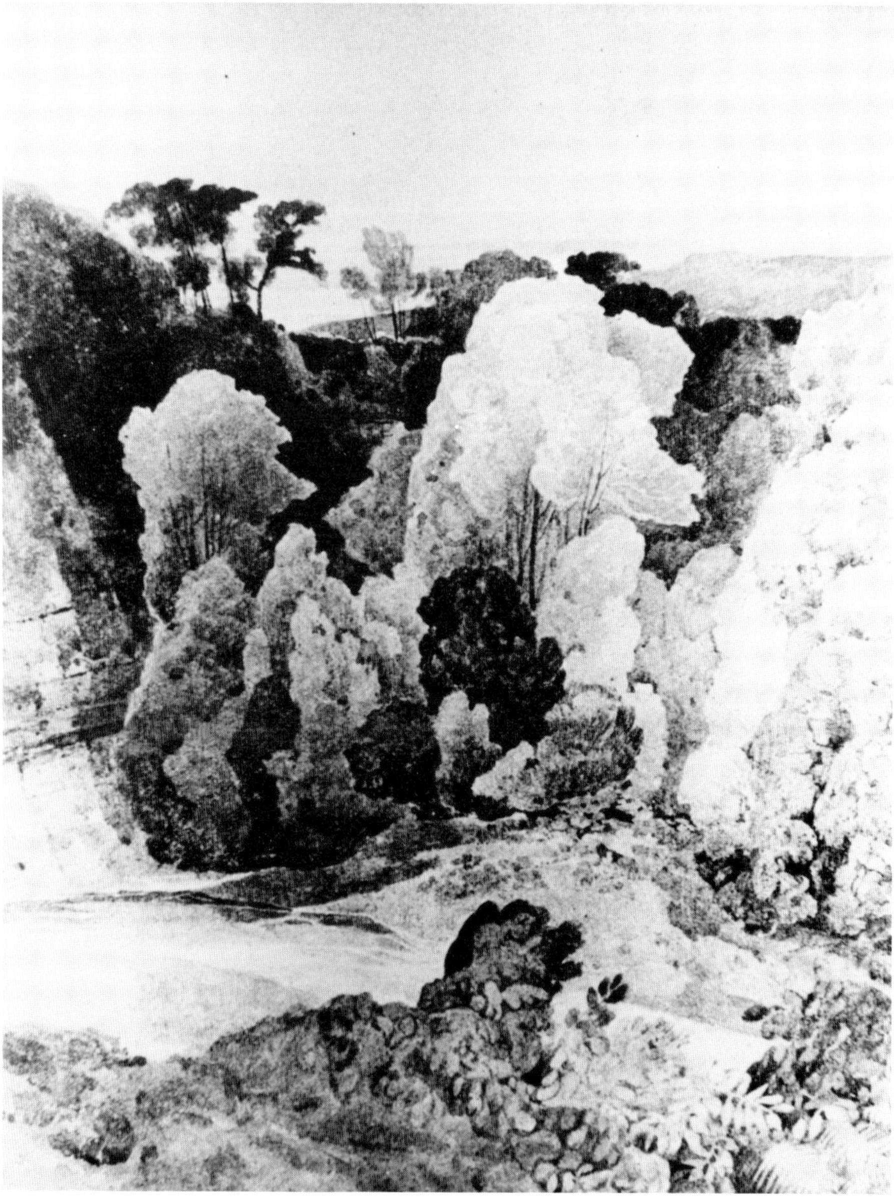

The Devil's Elbow, Rokeby Park
John Sell Cotman (watercolour 1806)

mastery almost magical. There are other drawings, one with a horizontal band of brown water and great dock leaves; in another a man is creeping up the stream, snaring fish. Still another is a study of a part of the bank of the lovely stream.' And of the best known of the Greta works, a symphony in brown, 'it is a scene of unchanging beauty.'

I love best his tree studies of this time as did Leonard Squirrell to whom, also, the period represented the quintessential Cotman. Such gems as 'Trees near the Greta Bridge' and 'The Devil's Elbow, Rokeby Park', 1806, working through the tones and combinations of blues and yellows and clearly produced directly from nature by the keen observation of the minute gradation of tone and colour in the trees, bringing out all the lyrical quality that so fascinated Kitson and other historians to say nothing of we lesser mortals. As I have said, the detailed drawing in the architectural subjects remained, given a new dimension by the more confident use of colour, but it was in these magical natural studies in which the beauty of the scene was always enhanced by the authentic feeling of the atmosphere of the day, that the unique mystical genius of John Sell Cotman fully manifested itself.

The saddest thing about the Greta period was the lack of recognition of this new Cotman. The public regarded many of the works as unfinished, his colleagues were intrigued but not particularly forthcoming although John Crome was undoubtedly impressed; perhaps Robert Leman was the only one of his circle who truly appreciated the quality of his work. The critics simply failed to understand. They were, in fact most disparaging about his method of painting trees and indeed continued in the same vein about his tree studies in oils of a much later period. As far on as 1824 the Norwich Mercury critic wrote (apropos of the beautiful 'Trees at Kimberley'), 'His watercolour drawings display a brilliance, clearness and accuracy scarcely to be surpassed. His pencil sketches are also superb. But we confess we cannot understand the principle upon which 'Trees at Kimberley – clearing up after a Storm at Mid-day' is painted. Acknowledging as we are most happy to do the power of Mr. Cotman's intellect, we are satisfied that he has some particular aim in adopting a manner so removed from the common course, and we regret to find that it is in this instance as unintelligible to the virtuosi as to the public. We were wholly unable to catch the effect.'

As Kitson so rightly comments, 'Its appeal relies on the delicacy of its constitution and the subtle tonal harmonies of its colouring. To the

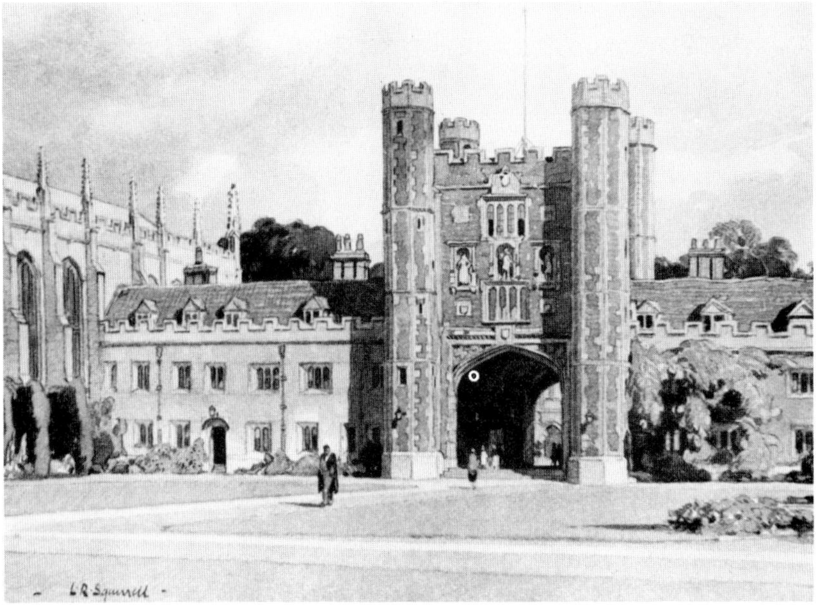

Corner of the Great Court, Trinity Colleg Cambridge Leonard Squir (watercolour c.1930)

modern eye (this in 1937) the picture seems to be simply an intelligent anticipation of future concepts: to the local critic in 1824 it was an enigma.' Kitson wrote in 1937; today it seems even more unbelievable. Not only is this method of working acceptable but quite normal; the feeling of trees can be better expressed by skilful juxtaposition of tones than by minute leaf by leaf drawing. Even Cotman's lifelong friend and patron, Dawson Turner, ignored those magical Greta watercolours while continuing to spend money on and commission more and more of the traditional work. That Dawson Turner could say of the, admittedly, very, very beautiful, drawings, 'His joy came from his free abandonment to the atmosphere of his surroundings and the knowledge of his complete ability to put on paper what he saw and felt,' but fail to recognise the even keener observation and strength of feeling of those charismatic watercolours remains one of the mysteries of all time.

Cotman himself, so far ahead of his time, can be forgiven the depression caused by the unfeeling reception of some of his greatest work. He even painted a collection of trees, trees and trees in the recognised manner to prove to his critics that he *could* paint trees to satisfy the popular conception even if not his own aesthetic sensibilities.

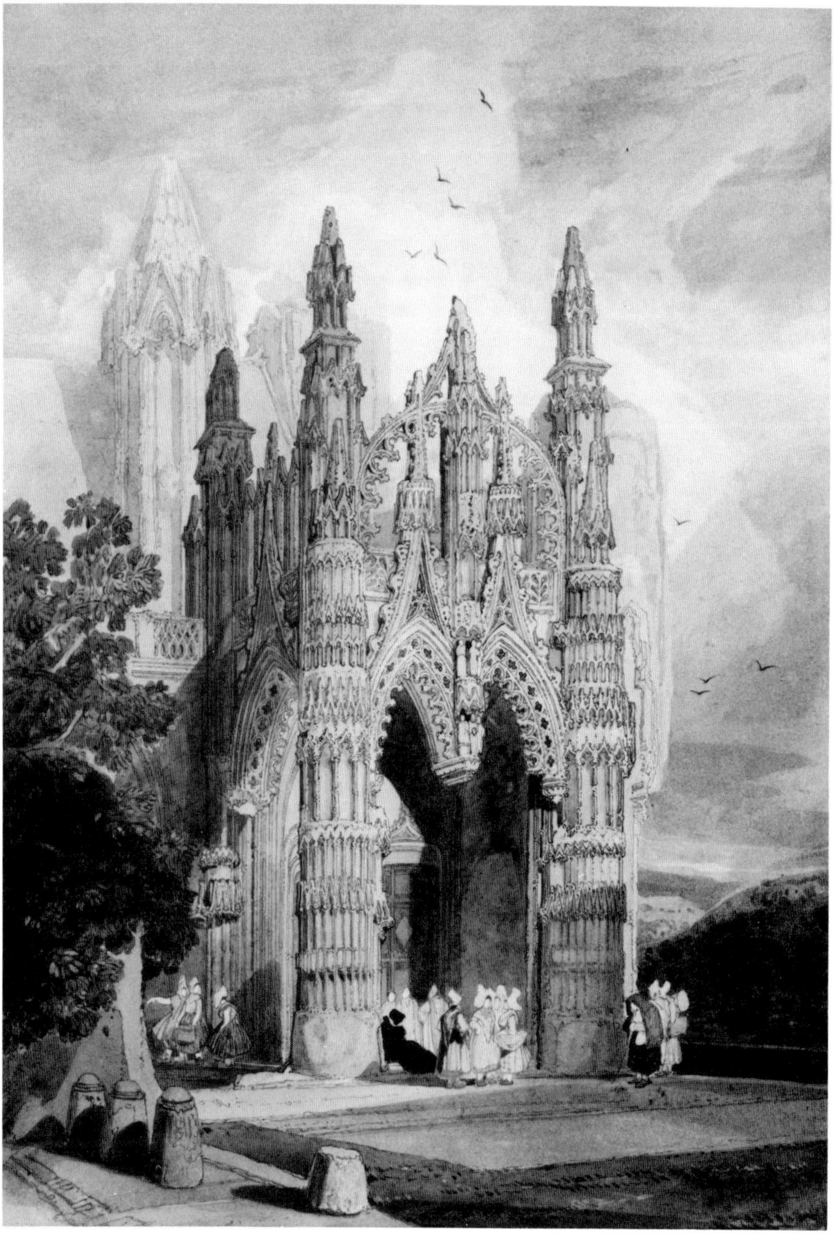

South Porch of the Church of Louvieris
John Sell Cotman (watercolour c.1825)

Briefly reverting back to that magical Greta period, it is both interesting and illuminating to consider the feelings of other art historians especially those more modern even than Kitson.

Graham Reynolds (1950) – 'The finest of all Cotman's watercolours are connected with this stay of his at the River Greta, for instance his 'Greta Bridge', now in the British Museum, and 'Drop Gate, Duncombe Park.' These are drawings in which everything inessential is ruthlessly supressed and yet every nuance of the scene is there. In them Cotman adjoins to his perfectly controlled washes a deep and vivid sense of colour and harmony.'

Oppé (1923) refers also to the 'Scotsman's Stone' and the 'various tree studies' as exhibiting '. . . one of the most characteristic and perhaps the finest of Cotman's many styles. It is not merely that his colour is at its choicest, especially in the rich tonal depths of the water, that the absence of elaborated drawing leaves the washes clear and clean, with the Japanese delight in transparent tone which Mr Binyon rightly applauds, least of all that the sober colours adequately represent the modesty and variety of Nature's hues. Over and above all this, his firm drawing builds the masses of colour into a balanced and contrasted pattern and the strength and variety of Nature are thus comprised into an intricate yet convincingly simple structure.'

Rajnai and Althorpe (1979) maintain that Cotman's month in the area resulted in 'one of the finest series of watercolours in the history of European watercolour painting,' and 'A number of these works are painted on sizeable sheets of thin and relatively fragile paper, executed with washes of exquisite control. The materials and techniques of the studio combine to recreate his earlier direct response to the forms of Nature.' Of 'The Devil's Elbow, Rokeby Park,' described by Andrew Moore (1982) as 'one of the finest of the inspired Greta drawings,' they write, 'It is without doubt one of (Cotman's) greatest drawings and one of the most original contributions to European art of its time.' If only John Sell Cotman could have known. . .

Looking at a watercolour of Leonard Squirrell's painted in France in 1927 – 'The Road to Gorbio' – I saw those Greta trees again. They can only have been unintentionally Greta, a far cry from the winding mountain road up to the hill village with the blue sea in the background. The trees in the foreground are almost incidental yet there they are, leading one into the picture, beautiful blue, green, ochre washes, muted but tonally perfect, juxtaposed in such a way that those trees become alive. They are so different to East Anglian trees that the

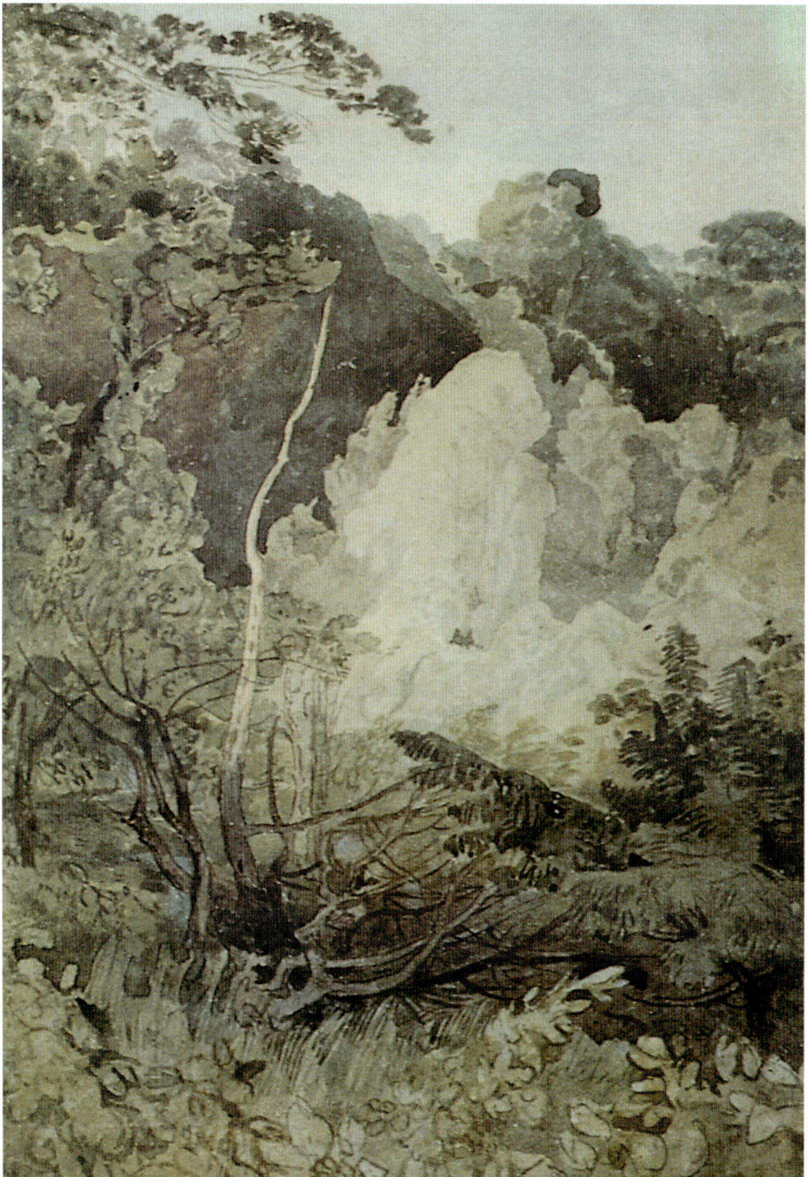

Trees near the Greta River
John Sell Cotman (watercolour c.1806)

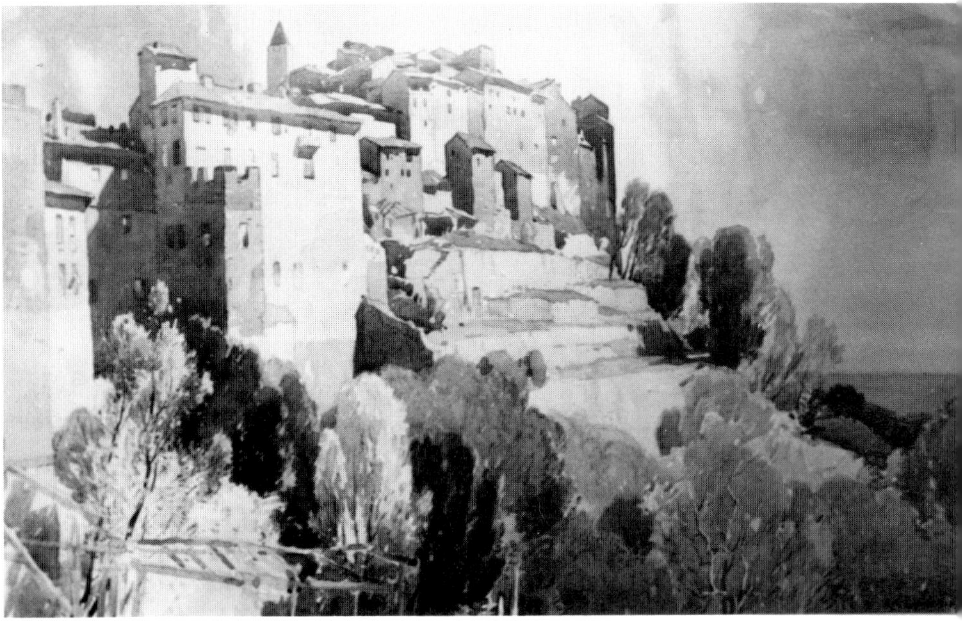

technique also had to be different; from somewhere in the depths of the subconscious, in this case undoubtedly intuitively, came the inspiration for those trees. Influence – yes, conscious influence – no, a classic example of the way in which ones subconscious mind, particularly that of an artist, retains any earlier visual impact that has made a particular and lasting impression.

The Road to Gorbio Leonard Squir (watercolour 1957)

* *

Like Leonard Squirrell, John Sell Cotman continued to draw throughout his whole artistic career other than during those periods of such complete depression that he could do nothing. From the earliest days of his teaching until those last years of his life as Drawing Master at Kings College, a prestigous appointment which pleased him greatly, he made hundreds of drawings* for his pupils to copy as well as the many more for his own use and for use as etchings. With both Squirrell and Cotman, the line between drawing and watercolour was often hazy for their watercolours, in many cases, were so finely drawn. The exceptions, of course, were the pure watercolours built up with tonal washes of exquisite finesse, a skill that in Cotman's case remained unrecognised and unappreciated until many years after his death. Although Squirrell was innovative to a degree of which perhaps few people are aware, his traditional watercolours were much more consistent in style, palette and quality while Cotman, as aforementioned, had wilder moments when colour seemed to go to his head and the end result could only be termed brash. There are as many differences as similarities between the two artists which confirms their individuality outside the basic tenets of excellence.

Etching was a craft common to both of them – in quantity Cotman probably leads largely because of Dawson Turner's commissions for his books of antiquities and the two monumental Normandy works which necessitated, on the part of Cotman, three busy visits to the area in order to produce the enormous number of required drawings. Etching, of course, depends on drawing but in producing the plates for such mammoth undertakings, Cotman used assistants to help him with the more mundane side of things. Whilst most of Cotman's were straightforward etchings, usually soft ground which gives the mellow effect almost of a pencil drawing, Leonard Squirrell also produced some of the most beautiful mezzotints and aquatints that I know of. From start to finish, they were his own and a more highly skilled engraver would be hard to find. As mentioned earlier, he had received a number of coveted awards for his superb engravings.

Again, it all comes back to drawing and those drawings to be used for etching or engraving must not only be technically correct but have an even more positive 'atmosphere' than those spending the rest of their lives as drawings when simply a little light shading or wash can work wonders. While Cotman was working on the preliminary drawings to be used or, at least, selected from as etchings for a particular project, he gave himself completely to the whole enterprise; certainly the resultant quality reflected the total involvement. Cotman used to insist that, in his etchings, he was influenced by Piranesi but with what justification, with no disrespect to either artist, has been questioned by some historians. Perhaps in his classical subjects it can be detected but the very subjects almost rendered it unavoidable.

* *

* Cotman's numbered drawing copies are known to have reached 4139.

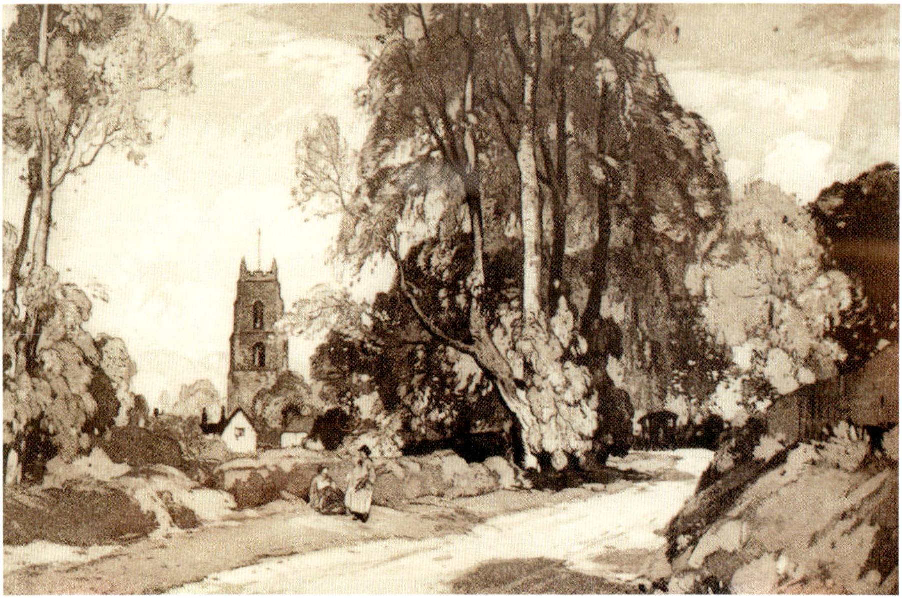

Stoke-by-Nayland
Leonard Squirrell (aquatint 1929)

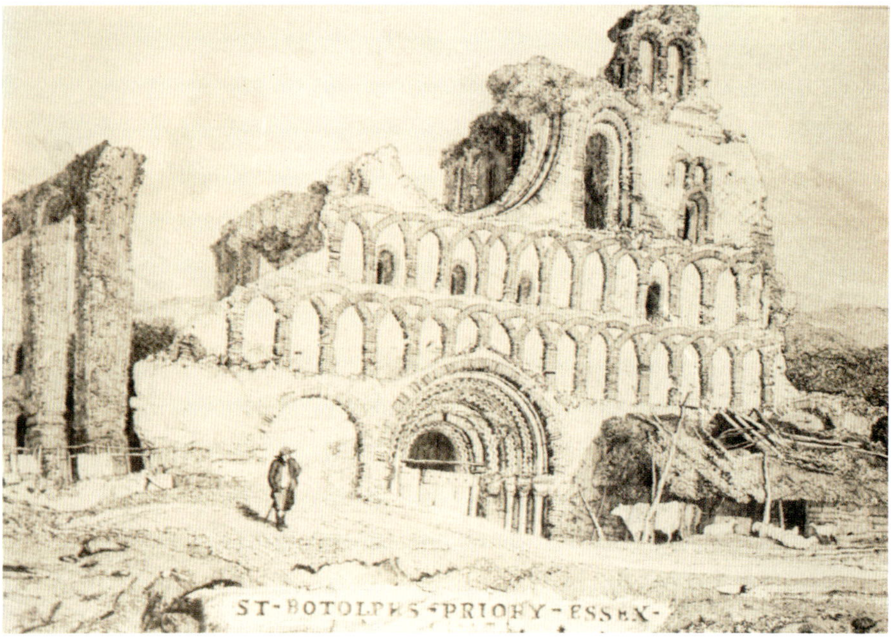

St. Botolph's Priory, Essex
John Sell Cotman (etching 1804-5)

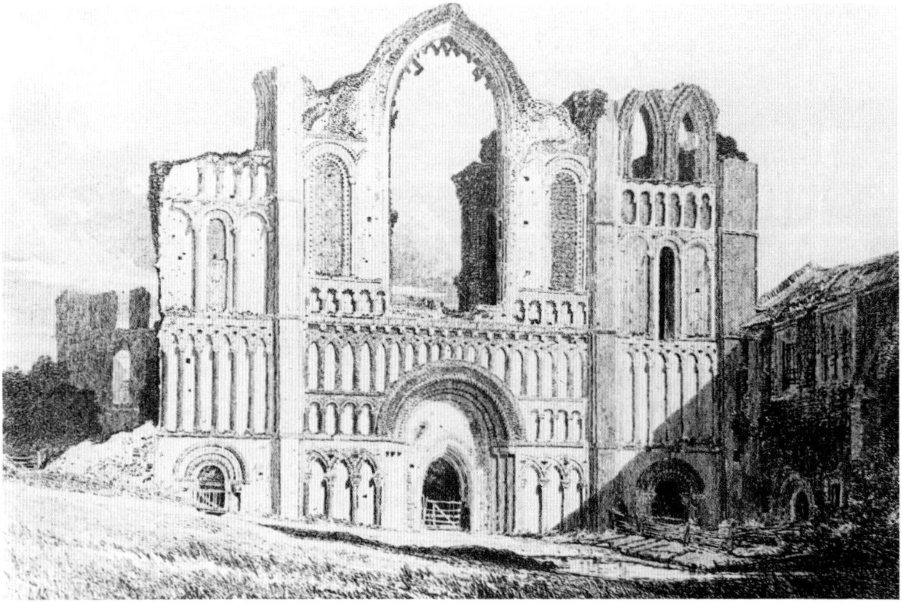

Castle Acre Priory
John Sell Cotman (etching circa 1805)

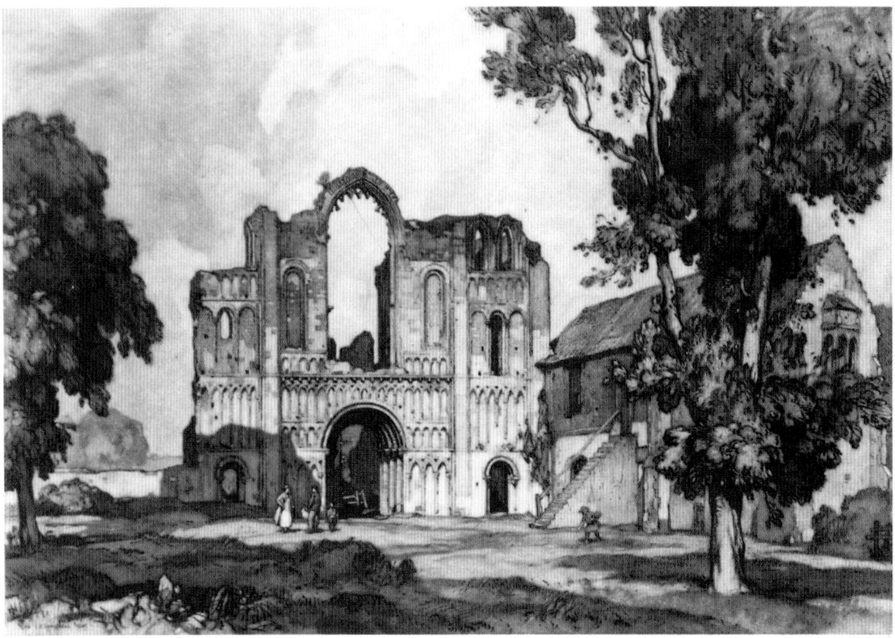

Castle Acre Priory
Leonard Squirrell (mezzotint 1925)

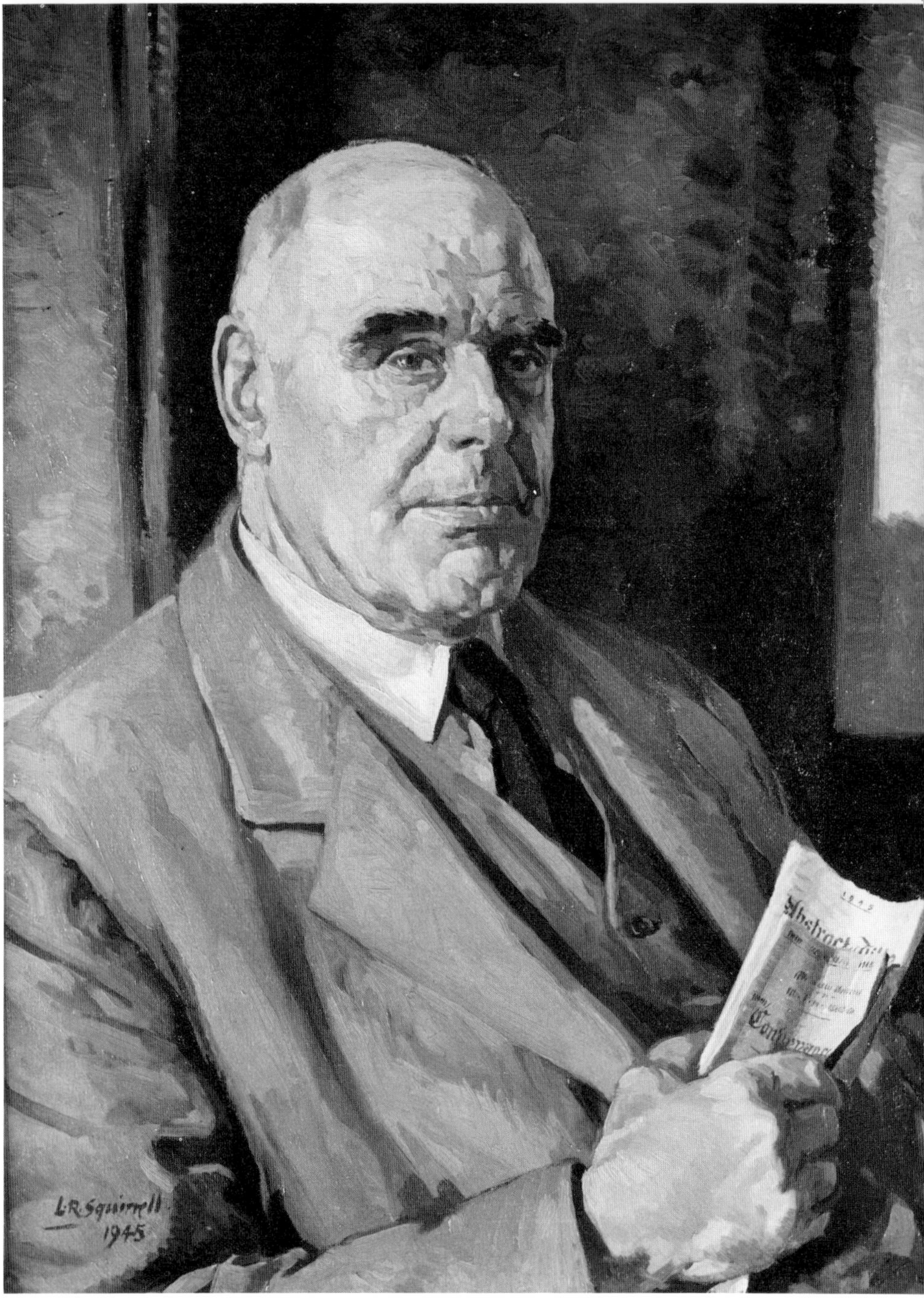

James Mason Martin
Leonard Squirrell (oil 1945)

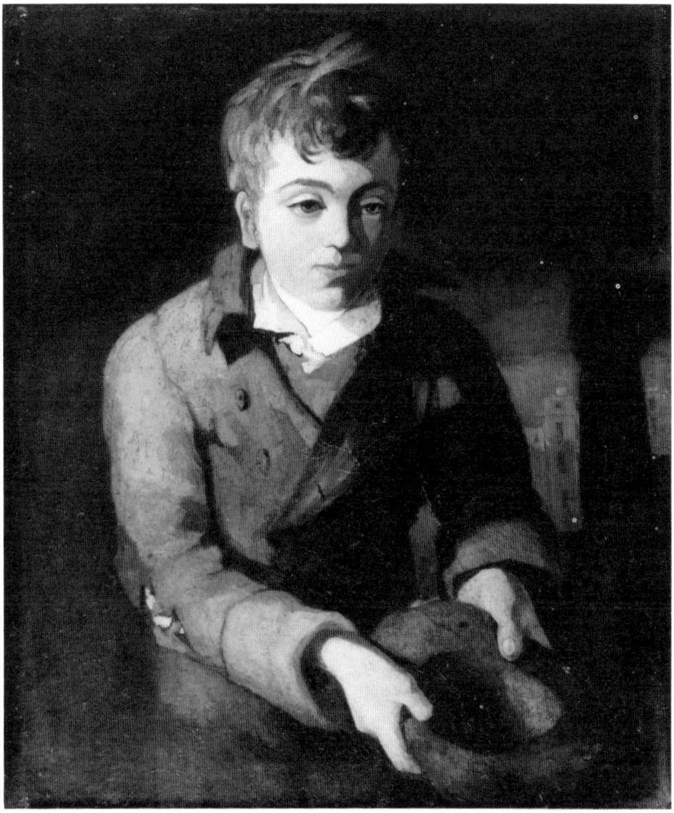

The Beggar Boy
John Sell Cotman
(oil 1808)

For a time, quite early in his career, Cotman advertised himself as a Portrait Painter. He was a skilful exponent of the pencil portrait and, having ventured into oil painting with some success, decided that this was an excellent and probably more lucrative medium in which to portray the human face.

The last thing Leonard Squirrell would have called himself was a portrait artist yet, given the time and inclination, the ability was there. From the pencil portrait of his baby son, Martin, to that of an old, old man at the other end of the scale, the few known pencil portraits are little gems, able to hold their own against any competition. Oil was not his favourite medium by any means yet the only known oil portrait, that of his patron, James Mason Martin of Framlingham, is a powerful piece of work, equal in quality to almost anything from a trained and practicing portrait artist. Never shall we know what could have been achieved had he put his mind to it more constantly.

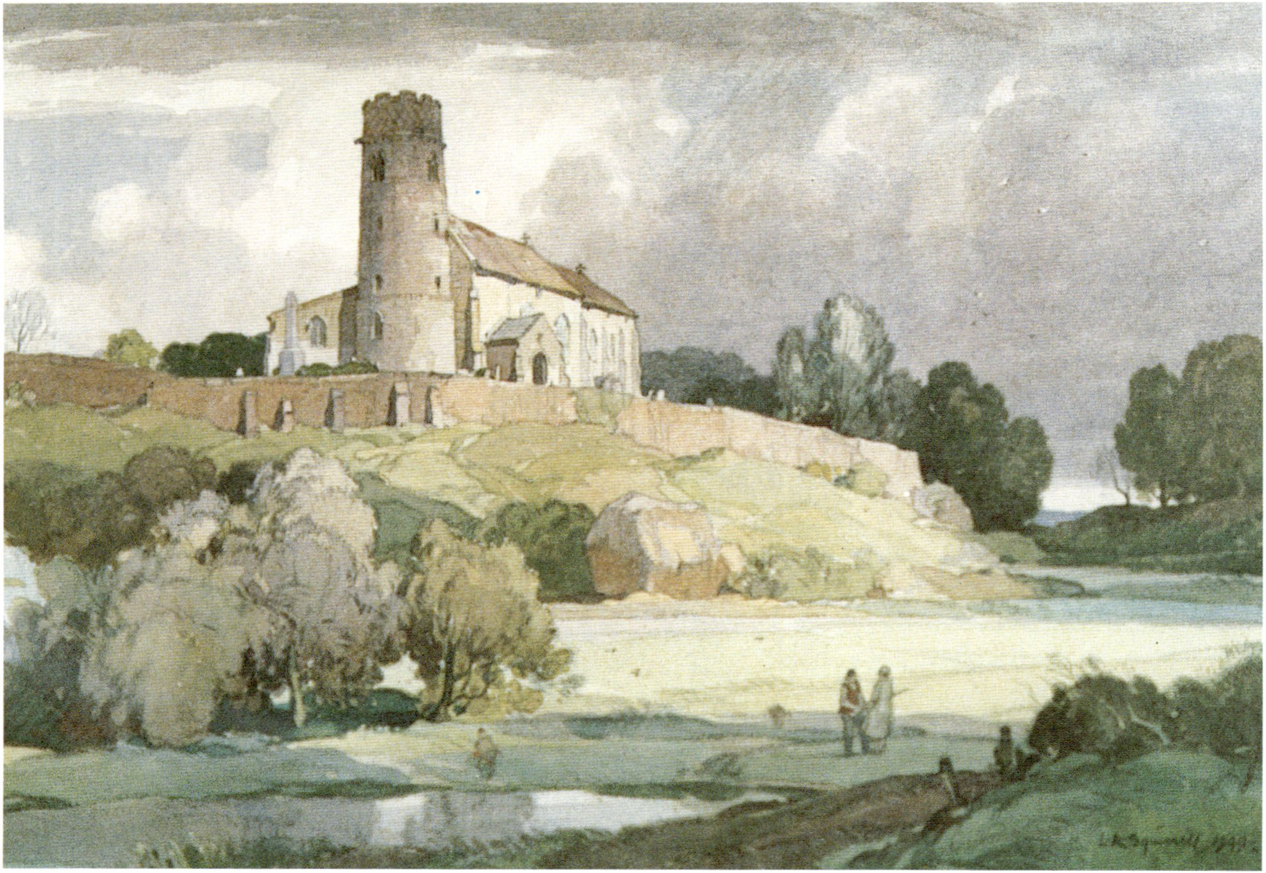

Haddiscoe Church, Norfolk
Leonard Squirrell (watercolour and pencil 1949)

Oil painting generally was more important to John Sell Cotman and during the three major phases of working in the medium, he is reported to have said it would not worry him if he never produced another drawing, and if he happened to revert to watercolour during an oil phase, the results tended to look like oils especially those worked with a flour paste medium. The comment about the drawing was not, of course, true but the fact that he could believe it even temporarily, shows that at times he became totally involved with oils. As will have been noticed, Cotman was capable of complete absorbtion with whatever he was doing at a particular time.

The quality of his oils was uneven although the unique collection in Norwich Castle Museum shows the accomplishment of his finest works. The choice of subject, too, is interesting, frequently being quite different to anything in his other media; classical subjects obviously interested him, also there are a number of important marine paintings, some with almost a Dutch influence, which serve to show the depth of his knowledge and skill. Was there a subject he could not execute in any medium with shrewd observation, artistry and his own particular panache?

Here again, it is his tree studies that, to me, are the most strikingly beautiful especially where his colour is muted and the expressive tones blended into a green and golden symphony. 'Silver Birches', c.1824, is pure magic, as Andrew Moore points out, 'the lyrical quality reaches its climax in this composition.' Kitson describes it as 'one of the most distinguished of all Cotman's paintings,' while Binyon sees it as 'one of Cotman's finest and most fortunate works,' and while not necessarily one to run with the tide of opinion, I can only endorse those sentiments. Running it very closely but sadly suffering the ravages of time and 'restoration,' is 'The Silent Stream, Normandy' of the same era whose composition can only be described as lyric poetry.

It is easy to think that only in the realms of drawings, watercolour and etchings can Leonard Squirrell be compared to John Sell Cotman but, as with the portraits, the skill was there, I firmly believe, to produce more than comparable oil paintings had he so wished. It seems quite remarkable that one who cared nothing for the medium could, if he needed to, come up with work of such quality. As with the Mason portrait, I know of several early landscapes in oil which are vintage Squirrell, totally competent and easy to equate with his watercolours. Then there are the surprises. Some years ago, I saw a large oil whose present whereabouts I do not know, but which at first glance I had

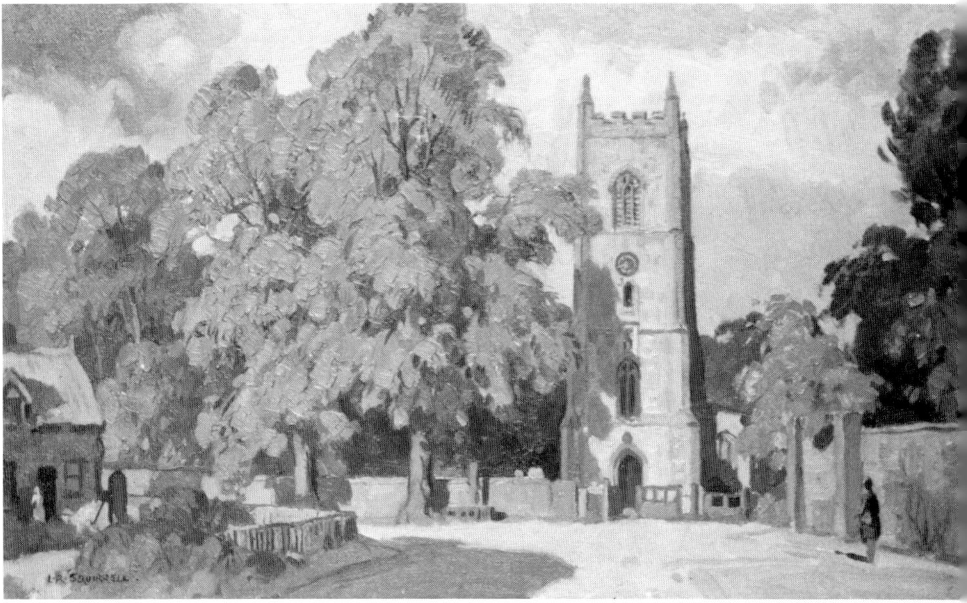

Lower Ufford
Leonard Squirrell (oil c.1928)

attributed to Cotman, and the late Michael Swinyard had a smaller but equally powerful painting of a sandpit wherein the medium was really *used* to express the multiplicity of textures as well as the subtle nuances of tones. Totally different, equally striking, is a magnificent rendering of a night train coming through the tunnel into Ipswich station – it is no exaggeration to say that one can hear, see and smell that train and the instinct is to draw back as it comes rushing towards you. The bright lights – the two large eyes of the train, the movement, the splendour, all point to the fact that, yet again given time and inclination, Squirrell had the same consummate talent and skill, the same ability to work in oil as in any other medium.

One thing that Squirrell never did was to resort to any form of minor gimmickry which Cotman did, often to good effect. Surely he had earned the right to experiment. Pastel appears to be the one medium not used, at any rate on its own, by John Sell Cotman while Leonard Squirrell gave much time to it and, backed as always by his accomplished drawing and unfailing colour sense, produced some quite magical results. Life was just too short for both of them.

Squirrell lived nearly a quarter of a century longer than Cotman but to realise his full potential, he needed another lifetime.

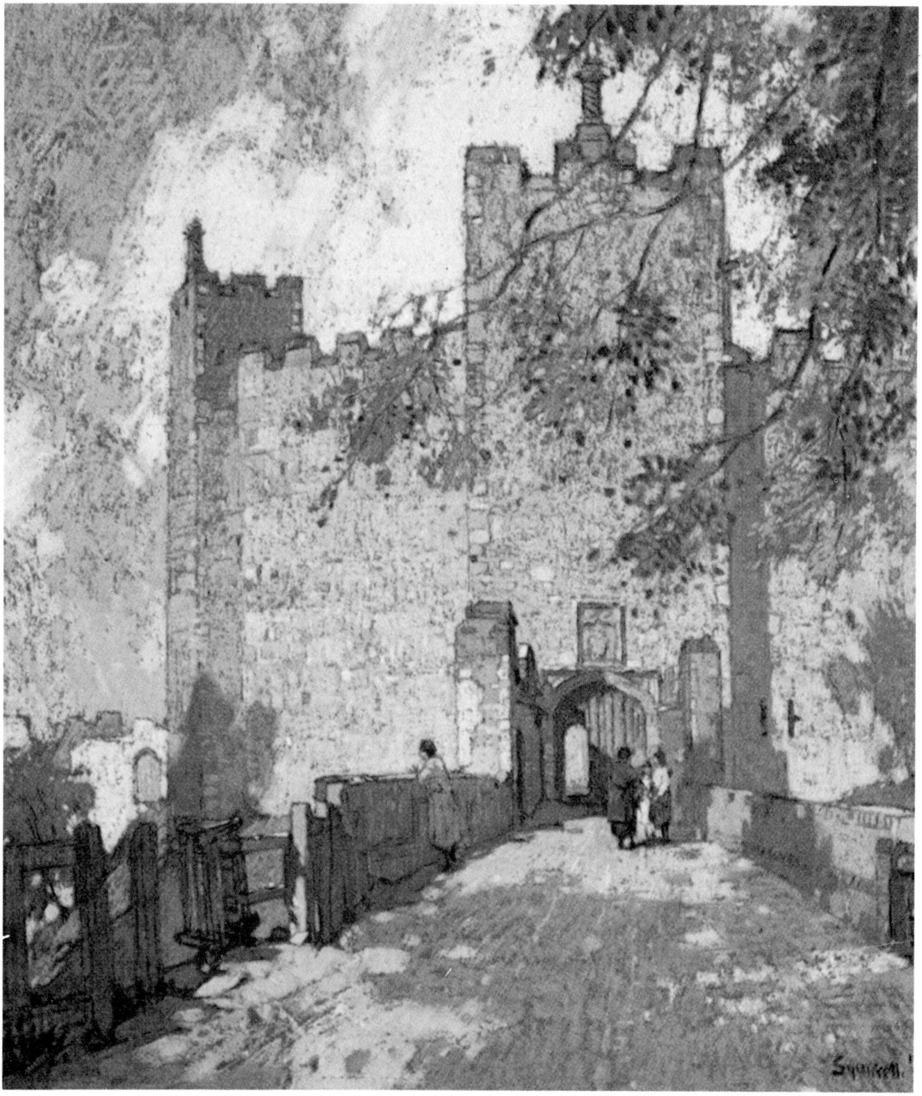

The Gateway, Framlingham Castle
Leonard Squirrell (pastel 1924)

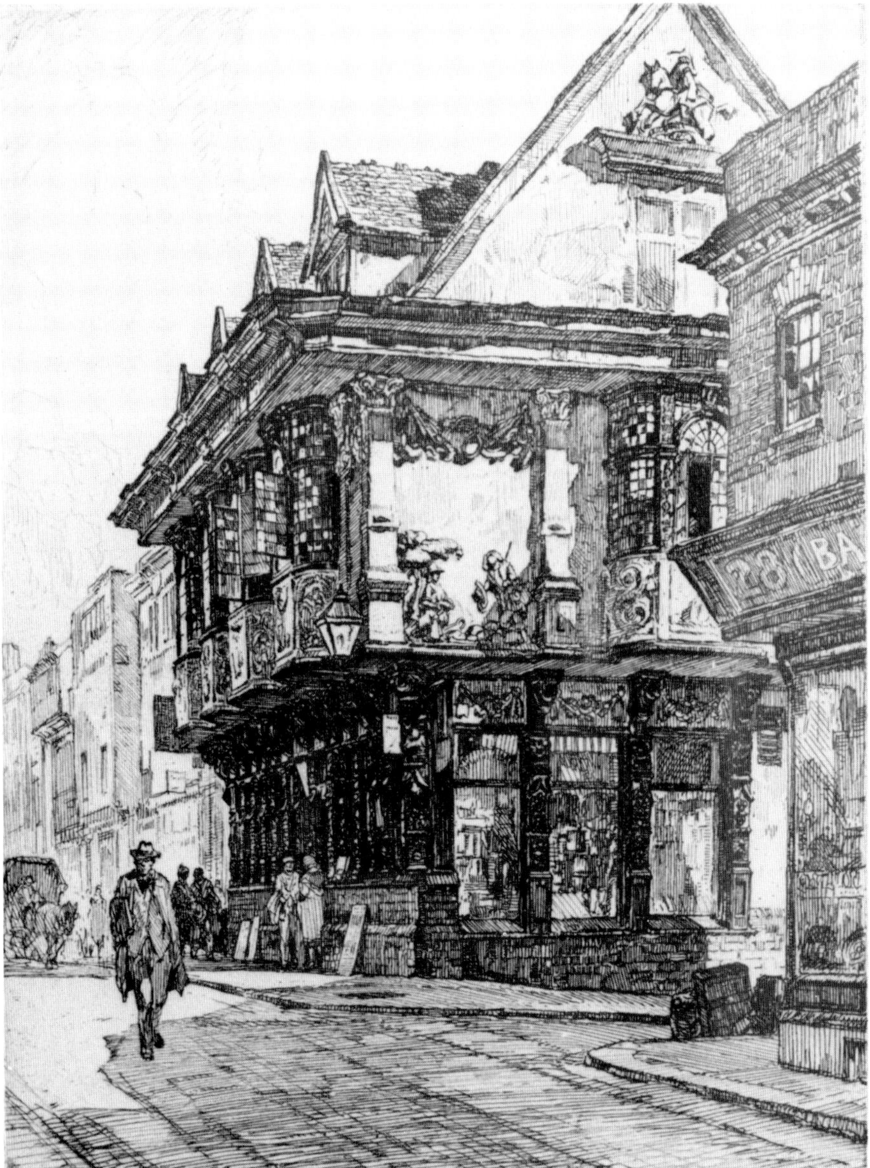

The Ancient House, Ipswich
Leonard Squirrell (etching 1930)

COTMAN'S PUBLISHED ETCHINGS AS LISTED IN THE JOHN SELL COTMAN BICENTENARY EXHIBITION CATALOGUE

1811 Etchings by John Sell Cotman otherwise
Miscellaneous Etchings 1811 (26 etchings)

1814 A Narrative of the Grand Festival at
Great Yarmouth otherwise
Yarmouth Festival 1814 (3 etchings & 1 softground etching)

1817 Specimens of Norman and Gothic Architecture in the County of Norfolk (50 etchings)

1817 The Nelson Column at Yarmouth

1817 Specimens of the Castellated and Ecclesiastical Remains in the County of Norfolk (50 etchings)

1818 A Series of Etchings illutrative of the Architectural Antiquities of Norfolk; with reference to the Authors who have described or Figured them. By John Sell Cotman, author of a volume of miscellaneous etchings and of Figures of the Sepulchral Brasses of Norfolk and Suffolk otherwise
Architectural Antiquities of Norfolk 1818 (60 etchings)

1819 Engravings of the Most Remarkable of the Sepulchral Brases in Norfolk (111 plates)

1819 Antiquities of Saint Mary's Chapel at Stourbridge, near Cambridge (10 etchings)

1822 Architectural Antiquities of Normandy (97 etchings)

1838 Liber Studiorum (48 plates, 40 softground)

1846 Eight Original Etchings (8 etchings)

Undoubtedly there were others not necessarily published in book form but worked simply for the artist's own satisfaction. It must be remembered also that many, many more drawings were produced than were used for the published etchings listed above in order that the right selection should be made.

To my certain knowledge (excluding Christmas Cards, Book-plates and commissioned calendars for which many etchings were made), Leonard Squirrell produced 93 etchings, 40 drypoints, 33 aquatints and 15 mezzotints. Again, although his daughter and myself have spent much time researching this, undoubtedly there would have been more. We have even seen plates without being able to trace the appropriate etchings and which we were unable to identify. It still remains a considerable achievement representing many hours of highly skilled and specialised craftsmanship.

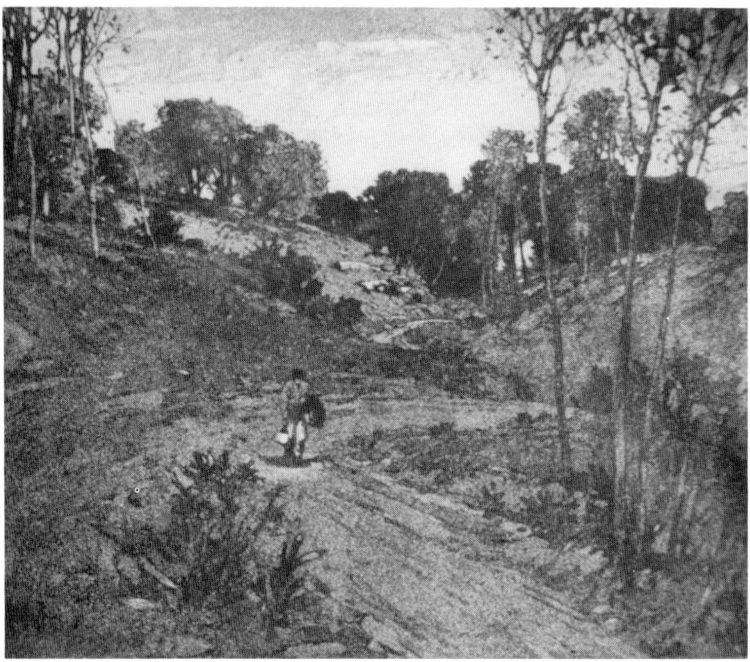

The Harvest Moon
Leonard Squirrell
(aquatint 1932)

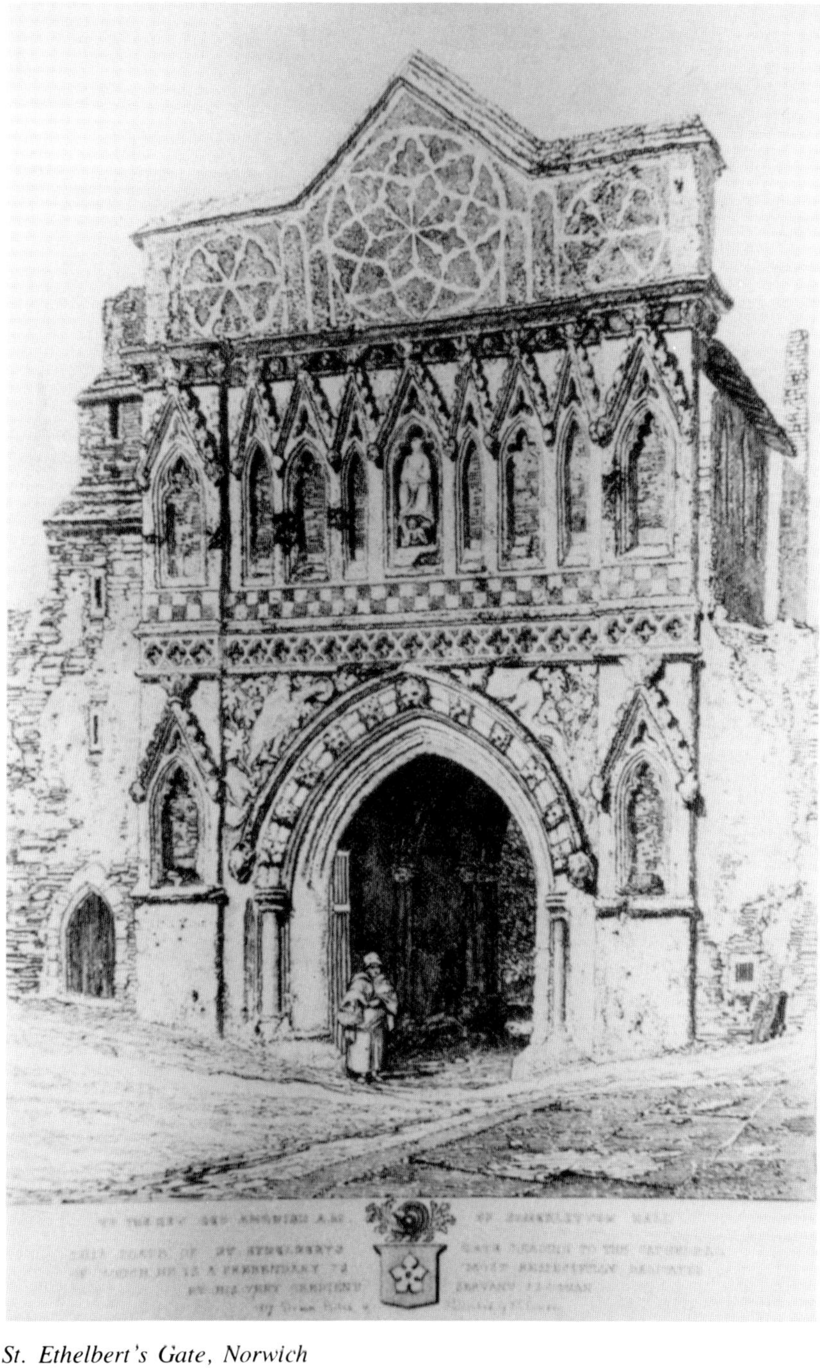

St. Ethelbert's Gate, Norwich
John Sell Cotman (etching 1817)

Chapter 5

REFLECTIONS

It is easy on the strength of some fleeting similarity to pontificate on the influence of one artist on another and there is, to my mind, far too much of this tendency on the part of some art historians. At times one feels that they are saying with complex verbiosity that Mailer was influenced by Dickens because he used full stops. No man is an island and every artist is influenced by many others, often by some almost subconscious observation later experimented with in his own particular way, in turn seized upon as his own inspiration to be experimented with or even copied by next generation painters. Influence and copying, even not very close copying, are totally and completely different, the former often unrecognised, sometimes attributed when not even there. Influence is frequently subconscious, drawn perhaps from something registered long before and tucked away in the memory bank of the brain, not to be confused with inspiration which plants an idea, a technique, a method perhaps not previously considered, often producing a result far removed from the original source. Neither influence nor inspiration necessarily produce results identifiable with the origination but, throughout the ages, both have gone on rubbing off and it is natural and right that it should be so. But, I repeat both are often subconscious, particularly influence – copying, unless as forgery, is usually patently obvious or acknowledged in one way or another.

Of course the Norwich artists influenced each other, they were working in close proximity often in the same environment, painting the same subjects, even being taught by the same teachers – it would have been inconceivable for them not to affect each other and each other's work. Yet, in spite of the common thread weaving its way through this unique group of artists there is little actual copying and plenty of individual expression. The 'deep unconscious bond' referred to by Laurence Binyon is a much more fitting description of the unity between them and, over the span of nearly two centuries, one becomes increasingly aware of this elusive bond.

And then comes Squirrell, demonstrating as though the years had never been, that same unconscious bond as if it was a plant that had lain dormant for years and suddenly burst into bud, to leaf and to flower. 'Influenced' on his own admission by John Sell Cotman, perhaps unconsciously by other Norwich School painters, perhaps just sharing that unique unity but, somehow, one of them.

Yet how different were their lives. True, some of them scraped a living by their art (excluding the wealthy Henry Bright who was blessed with the Midas touch) by selling their work where they could, accepting commissions, teaching or illustrating, but many of them were gifted amateurs working in their own profession, sometimes allied with art as Thirtle's picture framing, sometimes in totally different spheres, yet, whether full or part time, totally dedicated to their beloved painting.

Squirrell's was a much more down-to-earth approach, professional in the literal sense as well as in his work. When once asked if he had to wait for inspiration before commencing a painting he replied that he had no time for such luxuries. In the same way as any other professional man, lawyer, banker, doctor, he had a living to earn and a family to support and his life was as disciplined in relation to his work as that of any one governed by the most stringent rules and regulations.

By nature of his temperament, John Sell Cotman could never have been truly disciplined although when he became absorbed in a project, for instance the Normandy series or his early years as Professor of Drawing at King's College, he worked like the proverbial beaver. At other times, particularly during his periods of dark depression, he found it impossible to work at all. Undoubtedly others of the Norwich School worked in a more consistent way but one feels that their lives were, in spite of periods of real hardship in some cases, more relaxed and likewise their attitude to painting. Some, as aforesaid, had other, steadier, work which gave their painting, in a way, a more objective spontaneity but, whatever their circumstances, they were not faced with the pressures of twentieth century life. Leonard Squirrell painted his way through two world wars and the appalling recession of the thirties and, to his greater credit, kept his head above water. Both the solid reliability of the man himself and the exceptional quality of his work together with modest charges kept the commissions coming.

Even outside of commissions, Squirrell was a systematic worker. Days out, rare holidays, even business trips were seen as opportunities for finding new subjects to be transferred to his ever present sketch book. Many of those* sketches today would be classed as highly finished drawings, while a number were carefully annotated with colour notes and suggestions. A subject that appealed to him would be translated first, perhaps, into a superb watercolour, a pastel painting, maybe a finished drawing as well. Then it might, if suitable, be used as the basis for an etching or engraving but, although from the same early sketch, this would have a totally different character to the watercolour. Some slight variation of shadow might turn it into a different kind of day, some judicious movement slightly vary the angle – with dedication and skill this extraordinary man could work wonders from one small sketch, nothing was ever wasted and his craftsmanship was such that the need to abandon any drawing as unworkable almost never arose. It is interesting to note here that, albeit less frequently and undoubtedly much less methodically, John Sell Cotman made use of drawings that appealed to him in different ways and using different media. This adds yet another pointer to the importance of good drawing, for a basic sketch that was less than perfect could have no chance of successful translation, any minor faults would become glaring errors second time round as many lesser lights have discovered with despair and frustration. Many years ago W.F. Greeves wrote of both of them in a journal of the Old Watercolour Society Club –

'Squirrell is essentially a draughtsman, a superb draughtsman, it is this fact that is at the root of my attachment to his work. I have before me now two small pencil drawings he generously gave me long ago; one is of a footbridge at Blakeney* on the North Norfolk coast, how sure, how strong and clean is every line that matters, with a once and once only certainty; the other is of Cromer from the beach, a kind of

* Of these sketches, his old friend Fred Baldwin wrote –

'Between the two wars we went to Scotland on a sketching trip and in a short time covered a lot of ground. I well remember the speed with which he made sketches and notes to be worked up later in his studio into those dramatic landscapes that abound in Scotland. Standing on some precipitous bluff or a castle wall he would, in his admiration of the country beneath him, turn and twist until I expected him to fall at any moment. I am not sure that I did not sometimes retreat on hands and knees in abject terror.'

* This drawing had been used as material for an etching, 'Footbridge at Blakeney,' a copy of which is now in the author's possession.

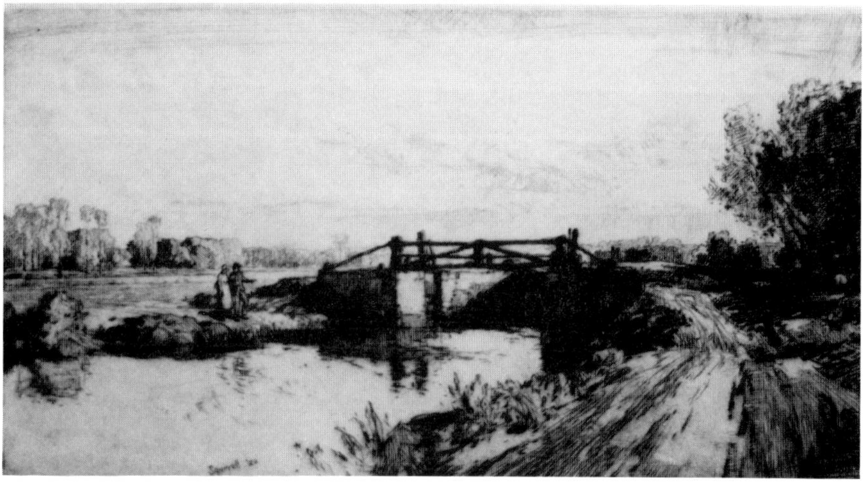

Footbridge at Blakeney
Leonard Squirrell (etching)

semi-microscopic marvel of exquisite drawing. As one who worked in the City of Norwich for forty eight years I am familiar with the very best of John Sell Cotman and nothing in the way of drawing can surpass those wonderful Normandy pencil and sepia drawings in the Colman collection at the Castle Museum, but these two little pencil drawings of the Norfolk coast by Leonard Squirrell can make something of a 'photo-finish' in a race with John Sell Cotman.'

Many of the Norwich School painters were also teachers of art, especially drawing, a way of earning a few more certain shillings than painting pictures that hopefully someone would buy – although Norwich was something of a cultural centre, the very number of artists selling their work meant that the jam was often pretty thin. We know little of the approach of most of them to teaching although there is no shadow of doubt that Crome, Ladbroke, Bright, Cotman and Thirtle among others turned out some very fine pupils, no doubt largely because of their insistence on good basic drawing, who in their turn handed down the knowledge gained.

Cotman we know taught mainly by producing vast numbers of drawings for his pupils to copy, no doubt backed up by helpful advice although one still feels that this approach is altogether too easy. One can only assume that his own experience with Ackerman's and the teaching of Dr. Monro whose pupils were expected diligently to copy, outline and trace drawings, gave him the conviction that 'teaching by copying' was the approved method which, indeed, can be remarkably successful for some pupils as far as drawing is concerned but is no way to teach painting. Again, as Derek Clifford has commented, Cotman's pupils seemed content 'to acquire as much as they could of his almost machine like certitude with the pencil', adding that this produced varyingly successful results although in certain cases, the female Dawson Turners for instance, some tolerable copies resulted and no doubt the discipline of these exercises was beneficial to all.

Henry Bright may well have thought to immortalise his teaching methods through the various instructional manuals he produced as aids to his pupils and others. 'Rudimental Drawing Book – for Beginners in Landscape' in six numbers was published by Ackerman in 1843 followed by 'Bright's Drawing Book of Landscape' in eight numbers and 'Advanced Drawing Book for the Pencilling of Tints' in six numbers. File copies of these books were held by Rowneys until they were, sadly, destroyed by a bombing raid during the second world war. I have often wondered whether other copies exist but have never been able to trace them.

John Thirtle produced a manuscript notebook – 'Hints on Watercolour Painting' – of some seventy six pages written in the once fashionable manner of across and up and down the page, rendering much of it extremely difficult to read. This book was presented to Norwich Castle Museum in 1950. Thirtle stresses the importance of working directly from nature and of minutely observing every detail of the subject. He writes at great length on composition and the correct approach to various subjects or parts of and, indeed, there is much information relevant to today's students if they can bother to decipher it. Many pages are devoted to colour and colour mixing but far too many of his 'recipes' contain the fugitive indigo which has virtually ruined the effect of many of his own watercolours. There are some good philosophies too that could be heeded to advantage by many modern painters – for instance,

'Remember, that when by the exercise of yr own Judgement, or the Observation of others, you discover any Errors in yr work, you Immediately sett about correcting them, lest in exposing them to the Public, you Expose yr Defects also admit not any self Excuse by persuading yourself that you shall retrieve yr Character & that by some succeeding work you shall make amends for your negligence, for yr work does not perish as soon as it is out of yr Hands, like the sound of Music, but remains a standing Monument of your Ignorance. If you excuse yrself by saving that you have not time for the study Necessary to form a good painter having to struggle against Necessity, you yrself are only to blame; for the study of what is Excellent is good for both Mind and Body. how many Philosophers, born to great Riches, have given them away, that they might not be retarded in their Persuits . . .'

I think there is no doubt that had it not been for his speaking difficulties, Leonard Squirrell would have done more teaching. In any event, he taught etching from 1925 to 1940 and, judging from the enthusiasm of the few survivors of these classes, was an excellent teacher, at the same time kind and firm, patient and understanding but strict and quite exacting. The written word came more easily to him though, and his books, 'Practice in Watercolour' and 'Landscape Painting in Pastel,' should be required reading for all students of those media.

In 'Practice in Watercolour' he describes in detail his methods of starting, using a small notebook and containing within its limits such areas of landscape required to make the subsequent picture. Like Thirtle he advocates working entirely from nature (as he did for many years) for students, at the same time admitting that he found it worked better for him to use his annotated outdoor sketches as a basis for studio work supplemented, I might add, by a prodigious visual memory. As could be expected, he stresses the importance of good basic drawing, also of progressing through the important half-way house of monochrome drawing and painting, devoting much time to this exercise before tackling colour as such. He cites Rembrandt's monochrome drawings revealing 'his remarkable grasp of tonal beauty' when he uses a combination of pen or brush line and wash but no (unnecessary) colour, and Cotman's monochrome drawings (for example, the Normandy drawings) especially those works in 'pure' monochrome 'where he dispenses with any apparent line, and building up a pattern of fat tones in frank, clean-edged shapes, with a peculiarly beautiful texture due to the extreme directness of the washes – rather suggestive of an aquatint in quality.' John Crome occasionally worked in monochrome and even his masterly 'The Mill Wheel' was originally made entirely in grey tones with colour added later, a technique dating back to the late sixteenth century.

Squirrell takes his readers through the studio chores preparatory to indoor working and elaborates on equipment and light; he also discusses painting out of doors, its advantages and pitfalls. Always, here unlike many teachers, he emphasises the fact that, having mastered certain basic essentials, the character of a painting should be the artist's own, the development of a personal individuality within sensible limits adds charisma to a work that is technically correct in every aspect, and distinguishes the true artist from the 'good amateur.' It is not enough, however, to develop an individual style, there must be sufficient variation within that style to maintain a freshness in ones work. In The Studio magazine in 1932 he wrote, 'Very important, I feel, is the power of varying ones subject, ones colour scheme and ones method of approach and treatment, according to the subject: of avoiding a constant formula by which ones work is instantly and rather tiresomely recognised.'

One is tempted to comment here that, although neither of them could be accused of following a constant formula, the works of Leonard Squirrell as with John Sell Cotman in particular and certain other artists of the Norwich School, are usually instantly recognisable but I do not find this at all tiresome, simply a tribute to their versatility together with strength of character and the personal genius that lifts them above the rest so that recognition comes naturally, be it, for example, one of Cotman's wild, restless oils or a 'schoolmasterish' drawing, a masterly oil such as Squirrell's portrait of James Mason Martin or a tiny landscape pencil sketch.

Before taking his readers through the construction of a simple watercolour with warnings of the many pitfalls likely to be encountered on the way to smooth completion of a worthwhile painting, he touches on the treatment of trees which takes us back to the discussion of Cotman's Greta trees in the previous chapter and proves that, while as exemplified, Squirrell used this technique from time to time, there was no blind following however much he might admire the Greta paintings in their own situation. He would only use any method where it suited his required end result, not because he admired it for its own sake. Like Cotman, Squirrell's treatment of trees changed with the trees themselves – therein lies their magic.

He cites the 'chunky' tree form that can be dealt with in terms of light and shadow, the thin feathery tree when a tracery of leaves is seen against the sky that is, to anyone clever enough, best dealt with by 'dragged' colour, a technique perfected by Harpignies, the wash technique applied to a mass of trees and the use of light and shade to suggest their shapes and form and the occasional need for the use of painted leaves to make a point.* In the room with me now, I have three Squirrell watercolours wherein the trees could not be more different yet, at one glance, they are identifiable as Squirrell's trees. If I was lucky enough to have three equally diverse Cotman watercolours, no doubt the same could be said...

Influences, teaching, inspiration, opportunity, talent – so many factors go into the making of an artist but, with just a few of them, there seems to have been some magic at work. They have been endowed with great gifts and the ability to exploit these gifts to the full for the enjoyment and enrichment of the lives of those with eyes to see and the will to understand their contribution to the beauty and grace of a wonderful world. Sadly, and this applies most of all to John Sell Cotman, they so often have to die for the rest of us to wake up.

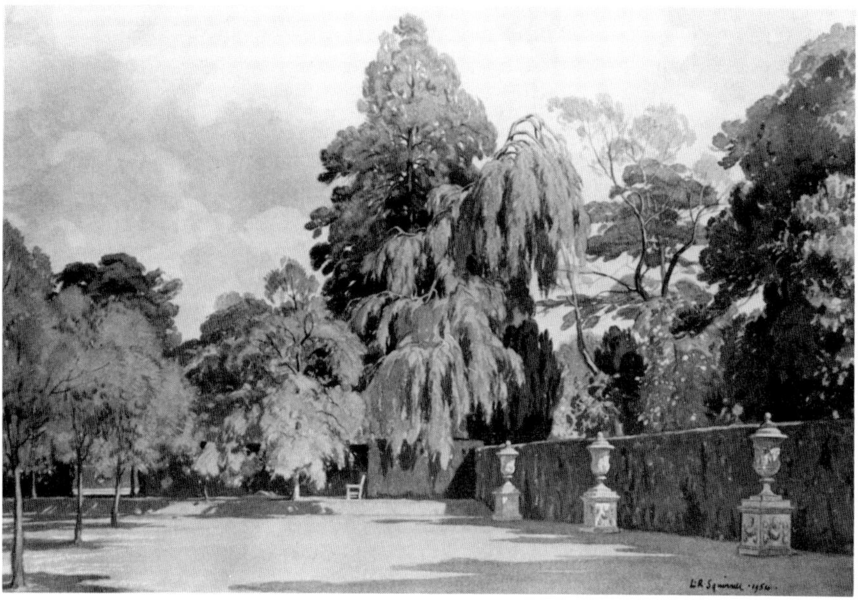

Anglesey Abbey
Leonard Squirrell (watercolour 1954)

* The most striking examples in one collection of Squirrell's 'tree techniques' can be found in the series of watercolours depicting the grounds of Anglesey Abbey commissioned by the late Lord Fairhaven. It is hard to think of anywhere that could have presented more of a challenge for the variety of tree species seems almost endless.

Chapter 6

FURTHER 'INFLUENCES'

In an earlier book on Leonard Squirrell,* Geoffrey Pleasance, writing of his personal interest and the importance to him of Leonard Squirrell, makes clear his own interpretation of the word 'influence' which coincides quite closely with my own albeit differently, probably more lucidly, expressed. In setting down his thoughts and reactions to Squirrell's work, 'I must not presume to use the term 'influence' directly in this connection for I do not find *the single* word (my italics) appropriate when referring to responses and reactions which are still developing as I see more of his work and as I grow older,' and later, '. . . for one artist to claim the work of another as an influence is, somehow, to clutch at the latter and to lay claim of ownership to him whereas, in truth, he belongs to no one person.'

As the late Professor Joad would have said, 'It all depends on what you mean by influence.' The reactions of one artist to another, the legacy of any one artist to *all* who follow him, the ideas and methods transmitted consciously or unconsciously into another painter's vision and language, or the inspiration to follow, to emulate in one way or another or simply to try out the same medium or method of working? As Geoff Pleasance so rightly says, there is no one word, hence the term (certainly in the present connection) is used loosely to be roughly interpreted as befits the circumstances and personalities involved. Leonard Squirrell himself admits to the special influence of John Sell Cotman, also of Girtin and Turner, but lays no claim to them. The 'influence' might extend to an occasional 'borrowing' of technique in the case of Cotman and possibly Girtin but in his own way. It is harder to recognise the influence of Turner in any of his watercolours, rather one should call this inspiration in so far as Squirrell's interest in watercolour started with Girtin, Cotman and Turner, in other words moved him, in the first place, to paint in watercolour himself.

As a natural draughtsman it would have been impossible for Leonard Squirrell not to have been influenced by Rembrandt and Dürer; he cites both as shining examples and, here and there, we can detect,

* Leonard Squirrell, R.W.S., R.E. Etchings and Engravings by Josephine Walpole, published by Antique Collectors' Club in 1984.

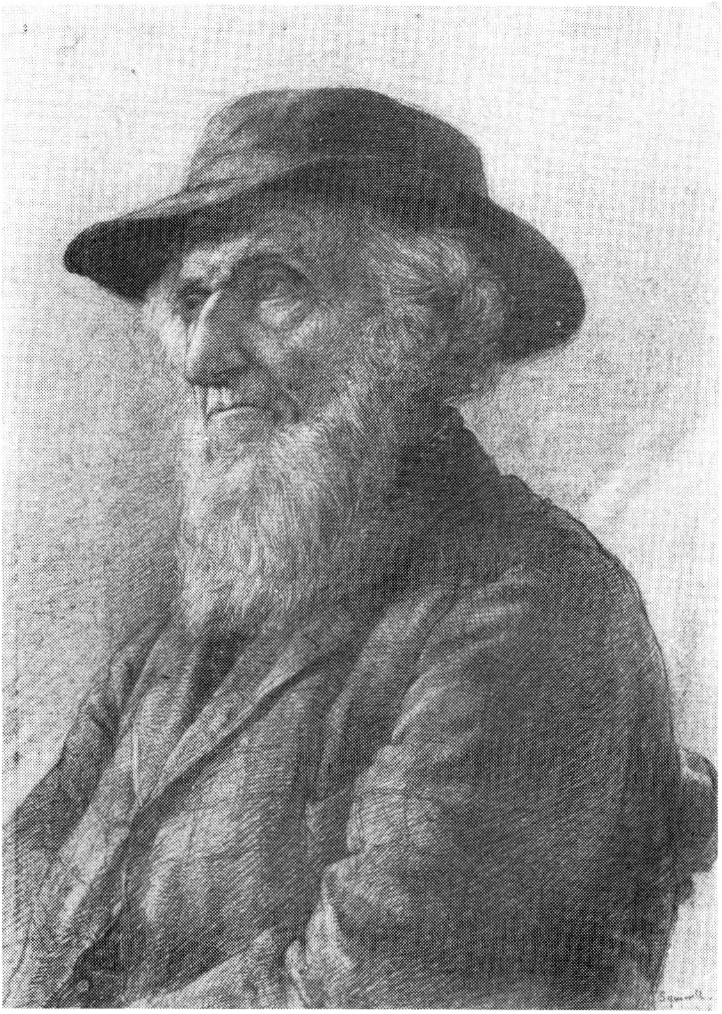

Pencil Drawing of an Old Man
Leonard Squirrell
1912

consciously or unconsciously, the touch of Dürer, particularly in his inspired pencil portrait of a very old man. Maybe there is a hint of Rembrandt there too but, again, how many perfectionist draughtsmen including those of the Norwich School, have not to some extent been influenced or inspired by Rembrandt, Dürer and Leonardo? How could it be otherwise?

Looked at in this way, let us examine briefly other real or imaginary influences, using the term in its broadest sense, on Squirrell's work. At the risk of laying myself open to my own criticism of the wilder imagination of certain art historians and of repeating inferences made in a broader chapter it is worth contemplating the connections between some earlier painters and the Norwich School followed by Leonard Squirrell.

John Crome was a great admirer of Rembrandt to the extent that much of his self imposed teaching involved the painstaking copying of Rembrandt's drawings, honest copying for education's sake. The influence of the Dutch Masters was unavoidable in the oil painters of the time, reaching Crome via Gainsborough and Reynolds whose work he admired and collected. It was certainly the combination of Gainsborough and the Dutch painters that gave Crome his feeling for light and atmosphere, much more so than in the case of Ladbroke who, while consciously inspired by the Dutch, never lost a certain 'heaviness' which made his work rather oppressive. David Hodgson wrote (c.1850) of Crome's work as 'combining at once the plastic colouring of Ruysdael with the grace and light handling of Gainsborough.' Crome was, at the same time, a more natural painter than Gainsborough who, particularly in what Reynolds termed his 'fancy paintings,' relied much more heavily on his imagination.

The style of Crome's early oils suggests, too, the influence of Richard Wilson whose work is also said to have influenced Girtin and Turner. Wilson's work is characterised by his insistence on 'breadth,' the importance of which Crome also emphasised to his pupils. John Constable's work again has this feeling of space and breadth and Crome, like most traditional landscape painters including those of the later Norwich School, absorbed something from Constable, '*the* natural painter.'

Too much has already been written about John Constable and more exaggerated influences and attributions attached to him (and thereby to his many followers) than can possibly have existed except, sometimes, in a superfluous and totally subconscious fashion. He has been credited with complex thoughts, ideas and aspirations which I feel would have been total anathema to him, a straightforward, earnest man whose overriding desire was to depict Nature as he saw her in his own particular way, to express her wonder and beauty in his own personal idiom and to be recognised and appreciated for his individual self expression. Above all things Constable wanted to be himself and to avoid any form of emulation although, in his early years for he was a late developer, he was certainly inspired by Claude and Gainsborough and there may have been a slight 'rubbing off' of the Dutch masters until the over-riding urge came over him to be himself alone. Like so many others, he has been accredited with the influences of Wilson, Cozens, Girtin and Turner as undoubtedly most of the Norwich School artists more justifiably have been, but I doubt whether he would have acknowledged it. In any case, how can pseudo intellectuals writing today claim complicated insight into the innermost thoughts, ideas and ideals of a very private man whose communion with Nature was very much his own?

By his own personal and total involvement with the natural world he has inevitably bequeathed something to all subsequent landscape painters, even if he simply opened their eyes,* and his little drawings as a basis for paintings or in their own right have, like good drawings from da Vinci onwards, made their own impression on those whose main appreciation is of good draughtsmanship. Yet, by and large, they were freer than those of Cotman or Squirrell, it was their own inimitable character that appealed and perhaps added a further dimension to the vision of those who followed. Certainly it was his drawings along with his masterly sky and cloud studies that most impressed and fascinated Leonard Squirrell.

The influence of the Dutch painters, Gainsborough and Constable, through John Crome if not directly for Crome was in many cases the primary teacher, carries on in some measure through the work of James Stark, very much a follower of Crome, George Vincent who initially followed but later outshone Crome in many respects, the Stannards, his own sons, indeed most of the Norwich oil painters particularly those of the early years. Inevitably every artist takes from his teacher to a greater or lesser degree just as Leonard Squirrell owed

* Footnote: Sadly Constable's paintings have also been laid open to flagrant copying; most have been patently bad but unfortunately too many have been sufficiently competent to cause considerable confusion, sometimes with unpleasant repercussions. As long ago as 1845 C.R. Leslie wrote, 'I am told some of Constable's sketches have thus been *finished* into worthlessness, and what is a still greater injury to his reputation, entire forgeries have been made of his works. Multitudes of these I have seen and they are put forth, no doubt, in reliance on the little knowledge of his style that exists among our connoisseurs.'

much to the great Professor Tonks, John Baskett and George Rushton, but, as time went on, the pupils of Crome developed a much more personal style which, along with the Crome legacy, produced a further combination of artistic genes to be handed down and again combined with newer influences and inspiration – and so it went on.

The watercolourists were much more under the influence of John Sell Cotman and, through him, derived some of the legacy of Cozens, Girtin and Turner. That of Girtin was particularly important as a link between so many diverse artists and also Leonard Squirrell. Girtin was an accomplished draughtsman which was undoubtedly at the root of his appeal for Cotman and Squirrell as well as most of the Norwich School from Crome onwards. With J.M.W. Turner, Girtin copied the works of many experienced artists/draughtsmen at the 'school' of Dr. Monro who actually owned a large collection of Cozens' drawings. Altruistic as his surface motives may have seemed to his student artists, Monro also borrowed many important works from other collectors for these naturally talented young men to copy and add to his personal collection. The taste for copying having been instilled, Girtin set himself to copy the architectural works of Canaletto, Ricci and Piranesi (probably the source of Cotman's inspiration from Piranesi) then, gradually and under the tutelage of Edward Dayes, his work became his own and he developed his very personal style applied to compositions of his own choice and creation. While undoubtedly benefitting from his earlier disciplines so much did he and more particularly Turner break away from these early influences that they have together been acclaimed as the great originators. This is something of an exaggeration in actual fact – as Graham Reynolds points out, Girtin tended to step back to the methods of Claude and Rembrandt while Turner adopted a much more innovative method using his own particularly individual treatment of colour and light. The combined influence of these two on the Norwich artists through John Sell Cotman stems primarily from the draughtsmanship of Girtin and the splendour of Turner's colour even though the Norwich men were considerably more restrained. Both in totally different ways were masters of fine detail and this too must have made its mark on the young Cotman who followed them at Dr. Monro's as well as on those, including Leonard Squirrell, who followed him.

Derek Clifford has commented on the two branches of the Norwich School; as we have seen, very broadly speaking one could say that the oil painters followed Crome and through him the Dutch masters,

Reynolds, Gainsborough and Constable, the influence of all of these diminishing as time went on, and the watercolourists followed Cotman and through him Cozens, Girtin and Turner. On the whole the (mainly) watercolourists seem to have achieved greater individuality but, again, if they were inspired by Cotman as undoubtedly they were – Thirtle, Dixon, Ninham, Leman, Lound, Bright and others – the common denominator is draughtsmanship, the extreme variations in Cotman's style made him a many sided influence or inspriation* at the same time making it more difficult to attribute the connection. One can accept the theory of the two branches only up to a point, there was so much overlap that the branches frequently became entwined. Crome painted (occasionally) in watercolour, Cotman painted a great deal in oil, in fact most of the Norwich School artists despite usually displaying a certain preference for one or the other, painted in both media; as I have said so many times, the foundation on which they all built was good solid drawing even if some attained a higher standard than others. It is interesting to note that some of the 'honest copiers' often became more distinctive than those who might have spurned the idea. Crome, we know, copied Rembrandt but his landscape oils had far more in common with the later Dutch, while Cotman, the most strongly self expressive of them all, was brought up on copying. Most of Cotman's pupils outside the School taught by copying his drawings, were ships that pass in the night, no doubt seeking another minor accomplishment or recreation without having any real talent or ambition. The female Dawson Turners were possible exceptions along with his pupils within the school, the most exceptional of all being Robert Leman. He copied a very great deal of Cotman's work in his student days but, subsequently, became one of the Norwich School's most important artists in his own right.

Joseph Paul produced initially a number of pastiches of Constable, Stark, Crome and Cotman which have been sold under various attributions at various times. Later, however, he produced some quite characteristic work of his own, no doubt also thinking of his copies as 'education,' not necessarily meaning them to reach the market place. The combined influences of Crome and Cotman show in a number of the Norwich painters; John Thirtle shows elements of both albeit

* Clifford says of Cotman that it is impossible to isolate eleven distinct manners in his watercolours alone although he admits that this classification has only a rough validity.

remaining one of the most self contained of these artists who, in their own turn, influenced to a degree the younger Norwich painters. James Stark and his son, A.J. Stark, who was influenced more by his father than Crome, also show suggestions of Cotman while Stark's influence as well as Crome's shows in the work of John Berney Ladbroke, Colkett, Vincent, Sillett and so on. David Hodgson's work interestingly and perhaps most forcibly shows the influence of both Crome and Cotman, the first example of a very definite fusion. Reverse influence shows, too in some cases – it would be hard to insist that Cotman gained nothing from Thirtle and probably from Ninham whose work he much admired, probably on account of the superb draughtsmanship originally inspired by himself but carrying the artist's own hallmark. Like Leonard Squirrell, Cotman could be generous in his praise of other artists where he felt it was merited, in fact one can find no evidence of animosity or jealousy between the Norwich painters such as existed between Gainsborough and Reynolds.

Around 1809 the fashion for etching, previously discussed in a slightly different connection, added another dimension to the Norwich artists, no doubt introduced by John Crome who had admired those of Gainsborough, Girtin and Varley. These artists were widely admired and encouraged such artists as Dixon, Ninham, Stannard and others to try their hand. Here the influence was largely shared, each craftsman introducing his own variations, but it seems to have been something of a passing fancy (although overall a great deal of excellent work was produced) except in the case of that doyen of them all, John Sell Cotman, with the enormous output referred to earlier. Certainly he must have influenced others including Leonard Squirrell but, in his own time, he easily outshone his peers. As mentioned earlier, Cotman like to think that, in his etchings, he was another Piranesi but the historians are, understandably, less sure. Hemingway writes: 'Although his (Cotman's) ambition was to become an English Piranesi, and some of his early plates were influenced by Piranesi in conception and technique, his publications were really closer to those of his friend, the English antiquarian publicist, John Britton.'

Oppé opines: 'Cotman himself thought he was following Piranesi, as though unconscious that while the Roman was lavishing romance on the antique, he himself was endeavouring to clothe the Gothic in a more than classic garb.'

Leonard Squirrell has made no secret of the artists who influenced, inspired and interested him and while elements of these, quite naturally and rightly, show up in his work, the natural Squirrell excludes any thoughts of blatant imitation. Experimenting with their techniques, yes – but all artists do that, those of the Norwich School being no exception although surprisingly rarely can a real single source be recognised. I have a strong feeling that more often attributes are pinned that never actually existed, John Constable being a classic example. But, excluding direct imitation and copying other than as teaching – how much does it really matter? The important thing is the end result and should we not all gain, in art as in life, from the experience of others?

As mentioned before, Squirrell has admitted that his interest in watercolour started with Girtin, Turner and Cotman and many of the Norwich artists are branded as followers of Girtin and Turner and, especially the later artists, of Cotman. Squirrell's attitude is one of sound commonsense,

'I know I am in the company of a great host of artists when I pay tribute to the inspiration and delight I have received from this great trio – Girtin, Turner and Cotman. Watercolour is a peculiarly English form of artistic expression and these three are the stars in our long line of achievement in the medium. Since their day, and especially, perhaps, in our own time, one could name many fine artists whose work in watercolour may be studied with enjoyment and much benefit, but as satisfying and abiding guides these older masters remain indispensable to the student who is willing to absorb the utmost from tradition' and 'Girtin delights us by his grasp of the large and noble in English landscape, put down with a new simplicity and dignity; Turner inspires us in many ways by his amazing resource in the manipulation of watercolour; but in Cotman we see profound love of nature imbued with a quality of selection, a distinction of personal interpretation, which goes further than the mere copying of nature which was typical, generally speaking, of the day. In his work is apparent, more clearly than hitherto, the 'artist' rather than the scene.'

Squirrell also goes back to Cozens who is said to have had a major influence on Girtin, 'The student can nowhere, even in Turner himself, find a greater sense of immensity, majesty and sublime solitude, than on certain watercolours of Cozens. In the expression of almost intangible size and distance he transcends Girtin, and though very naturalistic in his treatment, is uncannily personal in his art.'

Turner he describes as a source of inspiration and wonder and if anyone is puzzling on a possible connection between Leonard Squirrell and Turner of the Fighting Temeraire (the image of a surprising number of people who should know better), let me quote:

'From the drawings made during his several tours throughout England and Wales – first mainly topographical and later more free and imaginative, then the wonderful portrayals of space and grandeur in his Alpine scenes and finally his absorption in the problems of pure light and colour as revealed by his drawings of Venice – the range of his achievement, both technically and emotionally, is so varied and complete that no student of landscape in watercolour can afford to neglect a serious study of his work.'

Girtin, Leonard Squirrell rightly comments, 'was much more restrained in his vision, style and outlook, but such lovely drawings as 'Kirkstall Abbey' and many others, expressing the spacious and noble in English landscape, and painted with broad washes of rich, sober colour, are classics to which I return with refreshment every time I stray from the simple vision of things which characteristises great watercolour.'

Whatever its effect as a result of influence, teaching, inspiration or that missing word needed to sum up the mixed, often intangible, reaction of one artist on another, Squirrell had certainly studied the painters he admired; he also cites as others who have inspired him Bonington, de Wint and David Cox, explaining his reasons, 'All these men had behind them, as a basis for their great achievement, unfailing industry and assiduous training as draughtsmen, proving thereby the value of close, observant study of nature in early days as the preliminary to knowledgeable and masterly breadth in later periods.' In the realm of monochrome painting, as well as Rembrandt and John Sell Cotman, he cites as shining examples Claude, Gainsborough and again Turner, mentioning particularly the latter's pen and sepia drawings, sadly less well known than most of his work, made as studies for the engravings in his Liber Studiorum, 'notice how perfectly Turner's knowledgeable drawing is co-ordinated with the rich washes of tone, More helpful examples of landscape *drawing* the student could hardly find.'

One of the most difficult of the Norwich School artists to ascribe influence to is John Middleton, taught by John Berney Ladbroke, Stannard and possibly Henry Bright, he was also a close friend of Leman and Lound. Perhaps one could say there was a fusion of influence from all these along with that of his mother, alternatively perhaps one could say that this talented young artist was, more than any of them, completely his own man. Certainly his style is that of a much later period, he could have changed dates with Leonard Squirrell and appeared to put both more chronologically where they belonged, If only he had lived to exploit his exceptional talent to the full.

On the other side of the coin, many artists outside the School even up to the present day have been influenced by Crome, Cotman, Bright and others, sometimes more so than those within, and countless more can claim to be followers of Rembrandt, Gainsborough, Constable, Cozens et al. Leonard Squirrell has himself influenced and inspired many contemporary artists, pupils and others, but, like John Sell Cotman, failed to pass on the indefinable charisma. We are back to this mystery. Derek Clifford describes the Norwich School as '. . . a community of artists who shared the common spirit of the time but who, inheriting a local tradition of fine craftsmanship in the visual arts, by learning from each other and by drawing their inspiration from the same countryside, developed a corporate sense.' True – but it is not as simple as that or as superficial, in any event they were hardly a community in the accepted sense, some of them living and working out of Norwich for many years including John Sell Cotman. The more we learn about the Norwich School, the more we learn about its painters and their work, the more we become aware of the intangible, unknown quantity, 'that deep unconscious bond,' extended perhaps to include, many years on, a Suffolk artist who discovered the secret but never told. 'Squirrell is different,' they say. Different to his contemporaries indeed, different in so far as all the Norwich artists have their own clear individuality, different but different together with the 19th century Norwich School of Painters.

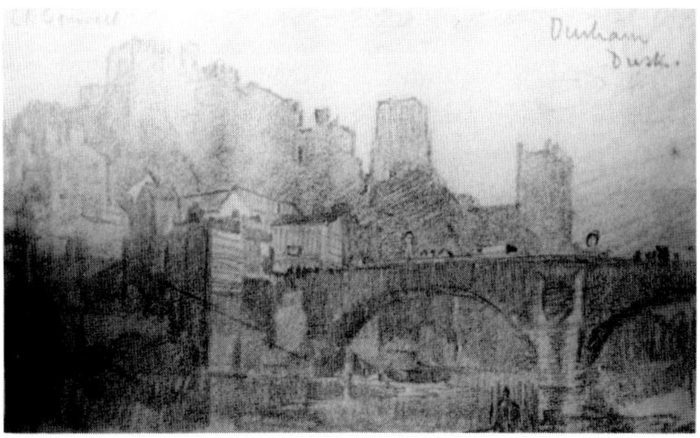

Chapter 7

'SQUIRRELL IS DIFFERENT'

With the exception of Harold Day's meticulously researched 'The Norwich School of Painters' in which he takes each artist individually, gives a brief resumé of his or her life and work and copiously lists all the known works, exhibitions and collections, most books about the Norwich School seem slightly to ramble, tending to jump back and forth and roundabout while exploring the relativities and relationships in all their complexities, at the same time expressing the author's own, always illuminating, personal views and preferences. In no way is that a criticism, all these books are full of interest because of the fascinating people whose story they tell. Only too well do I understand for, perhaps even more than the rest having introduced a further character to the scene, have I failed to present any sort of coherent, chronological study. I have realised and accepted the impossibility, feeling that herein lies part of the charm of the Norwich story, the subtle interweaving that brooks no systematic disentanglement.

The overlapping and spacing, the combined before and after influences, the relationships and associations, seem both to pull together and to extend – extend, too, over the years into the next century to include an enigmatic Suffolk artist who just happened to be born too late. There was always something about Squirrell's work that made it seemingly impossible to categorise, something was 'different' and that indefinable difference communicated itself to all sorts and conditions of men and women, young and old, professional artists and complete laymen. Was it not perhaps the more perceptive of these who queried in all three Retrospective Exhibitions the possible affinity of Leonard Squirrell with the painters of the Norwich School? Those not familiar with the School and the work of its artists felt the intangible difference between Squirrell and other 20th century artists of whatever persuasion but failed to identify an earlier connection.

In all honesty, I do not believe Leonard Squirrell saw his own work in this connection; aside from anything else, his inborn modesty would have kept him from identifying himself with such distinguished names as Cotman and Bright. Generally speaking it would be too soon after his death to be truly objective about a person's artistic endeavours or to attempt to assess his place in history, but some instinct has occasioned enough speculation, undoubtedly among those familiar

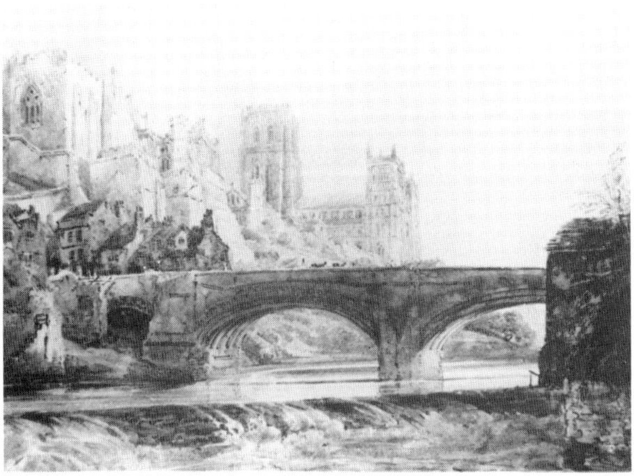

Durham Cathedral Thomas Girtin (pencil and watercolour 1799)

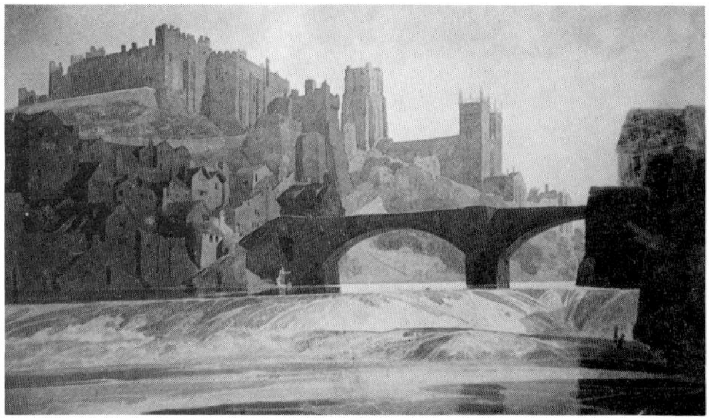

Durham Castle and Cathedral John Sell Cotman (pencil and watercolour 1809-10)

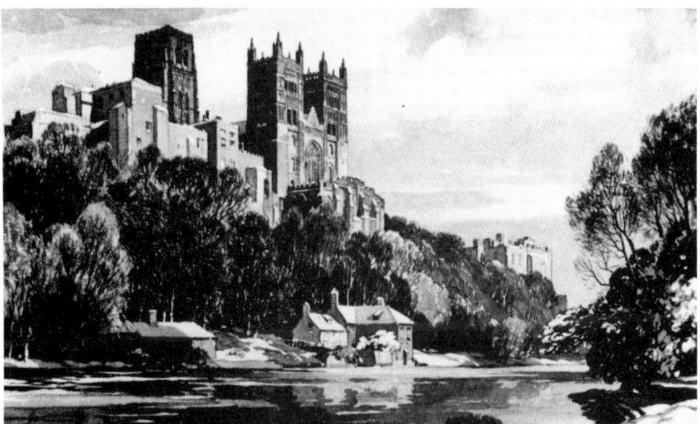

Durham, Winter Leonard Squirrell (watercolour)

with the work of the Norwich School, to prompt me further to investigate the suggestion and seriously to consider a more than superficial relationship. As W.F. Greeves observes, 'Everybody is somebody's child; the artist is fortunate in being able to choose his 'parents' although it is always incumbent upon him to be himself.' If, as he suggests, one thinks of Cotman and Girtin as the natural parents-in-art of this very gifted child who, like most children, inherited certain qualities but was very much a person in his own right, equally we can think of 'home' as the Norwich School. Perhaps in this context it would have been more appropriate to consider Girtin as a grandparent for Cotman (and others) were also his 'children' although his home was too early for and outside of the School, that extraordinarily diverse collection of artists with a strange, intangible empathy encompassing some elusive common identity. Perhaps, after all, this has little to do with the obvious inspirational forebears, the influence of each other on the one hand or the sometimes attributed outsiders (for instance Bourdon, Claude and Poussin on Cotman, Corot and Whistler on Squirrell) on the other, the mysterious light and atmosphere of East Anglia (for there have been many good East Anglian painters), but a unique phenomenon that we may never quite understand.

The more I think about it and talk to the people who can claim some authority, the more sure I have become that this so called 'difference' about Leonard Squirrell identifies him with the Norwich painters. Maybe in a hundred years time, more or less, there may appear another gifted throwback with this obvious artistic home but, for the moment, I feel in very strong agreement with those who choose to label Leonard Squirrell 'the last of the Norwich School.'

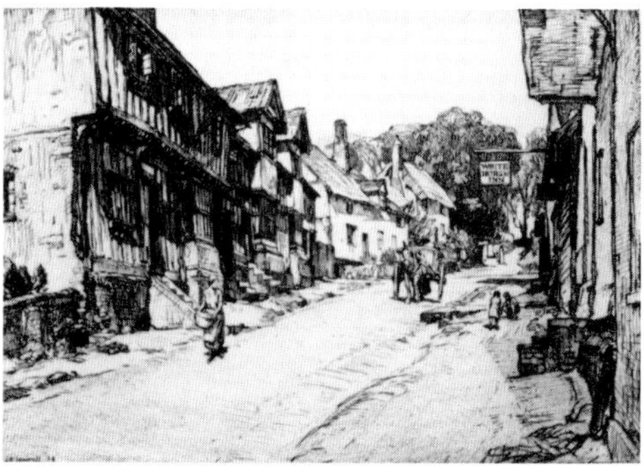

BIBLIOGRAPHY

'Henry Bright 1810-1871 Paintings and Drawings in Norwich Castle Museum', Marjorie Allthorpe-Guyton, *Norfolk Museums Service,* 1986.
'John Thirtle 1777-1839 Drawings in Norwich Castle Museum', Marjorie Allthorpe-Guyton, *Norfolk Museums Service,* 1977.
'Paintings of the Norwich School', G.V. Barnard, *Jarrolds,* c.1950.
'Suffolk Artists 1750-1930', Chlöe Bennett, *Images Publications and Ipswich Borough Council,* 1991.
'Leonard Squirrell, R.W.S., R.E.', Patricia Butler, *Ipswich Art Club and Ipswich Museums,* 1978.
'Watercolours from the Turner Bequest 1819-1845', Martin Butlin, *Tate Gallery.*
'Collecting English Watercolours', Derek Clifford, *John Baker.*
'Watercolours of the Norwich School', Derek Clifford, *Cory, Adams and McKay,* 1965.
'A Broad Canvas Art in East Anglia since 1880', Ian Collins, *Parke Sutton Publishing,* 1986.
'East Anglian Painters, Vols. I, II and III', Harold A.E. Day, *Eastbourne Fine Art,* 1967, 1968 and 1969.
'The Norwich School of Painters', Harold A.E. Day, *Eastbourne Fine Art,* 1979.
'The Norwich School of Painters', W.F. Dickes, *Dickes,* 1905.
'Watercolour Painting in Britain, Vols. I, II and III', Martin Hardie, Batsford, *1966-68.*
'The Norwich School of Painters', Andrew Hemingway, *Phaidon,* 1979.
'The Life of John Sell Cotman', Sidney Kitson, *Faber and Faber,* 1937.
'Dictionary of Watercolour Artists', Vols. 1 and II, Huon Mallalieu, *Antique Collectors' Club,* 1979.
'John Sell Cotman, 1777-1839', Andrew Moore, *Norfolk Museums Service,* 1982.
'The Norwich School of Artists', Andrew Moore, *Norfolk Museums Service,* 1985.
'The Watercolour Drawings of John Sell Cotman', A.P. Oppé, *The Studio,* 1923.
'The Norwich School of Painters', Miklós Rajnai, *Jarrolds,* 1978.
'English Watercolours', Graham Reynolds, *Herbert Press,* 1988.
'Turner', Graham Reynolds, *Thames and Hudson,* 1969.
'Master Drawings', Schuler and Hanser, Trans. Gillian Brydone, *Macdonald,* 1962.
'The Glory of Watercolour — R.W.S. Diploma Collection', Michael Spender, *David and Charles,* 1987.
'Landscape Painting in Pastel', Leonard Squirrell, A.R.W.S., R.E.,

Pitman, 1947.
'Practice in Watercolour', Leonard Squirrell, R.W.S., R.E., *Pitman,* 1950.
(There are a number of books, many of them now out of print, illustrated by Leonard Squirrell)
'Leonard Squirrell, R.W.S., R.E. A Biographical Scrapbook', Josephine Walpole, *Antique Collectors' Club,* 1982.
'Leonard Squirrell, R.W.S., R.E. Etchings and Engravings', Josephine Walpole, *Antique Collectors' Club,* 1984.

Although in a way incidental to this book very relevant mention has been made of John Constable R.A., and his work. For those interested in further reading, I will spare them a complete bibliography but list the books in my own (relatively!) small collection as a useful start.

'Constable Oil Sketches', John Baskett, *Barrie and Rockliff.*
'John Constable's Correspondence Vols. I, II, III, IV and V', Ed. R. Beckett, *Suffolk Records Society/H.M.S.O.*
'John Constable R.A. 1776-1837', Freda Constable, *Terence Dalton,* 1975.
'Constable Drawings', Harold A.E. Day, *Eastbourne Fine Art,* 1975.
'The Discovery of Constable', Ian Fleming-Williams and Leslie Parris, *Hamish Hamilton,* 1984.
'Constable and his World', Reg Gadney, *Thames and Hudson,* 1976.
'Constable', Guisepe Gatt, *Thames and Hudson,* 1968.
'Constable and the Critics 1802-1837', June Crosby Ivy, *Boydell Press,* 1991.
'Memoirs of the Life of John Constable', C.R. Leslie, *Phaidon,* 1951 Edn.
'Constable Sketches', John Mayne, *Faber Gallery.*
'Constable Paintings, Watercolours and Drawings', Leslie Parris, Ian Fleming Williams, Conal Shields, *Tate Gallery,* 1976.
'Constable', Leslie Parris and Ian Fleming-Williams, *Tate Gallery,* 1991.
'John Constable – The Man and his Work', Carlos Peacock, *John Baker,* 1965.
'John Constable', Pheobe Pool, *Blandford,* 1963.
'Constable – The natural painter', Graham Reynolds, *Cory, Adams and McKay,* 1965.
'John Constable, R.A.', The Hon. Andrew Shirley, *Medici Society,* 1954.
'John Constable', John Sunderland, *Phaidon,* 1971.
'Constable – Paintings, Drawings and Watercolours', Basil Taylor, *Phaidon,* 1973.

INDEX

Allthorpe-Guyton, Marjorie, 29, 72

Binyon, Lawrence, 17, 61, 72, 81, 88
Bright, Henry, 18, 24, 43, 44, 52, 57, 61, 89, 91, 92, 101, 104, 105, 106
British Museum, 49, 50, 67

Cheetham, Francis, 29
Clifford, Derek, 41, 43, 46, 49, 58, 92, 100, 101, 105
Clover, Joseph, 24
Colkett, Samuel David, 39
Constable, John, R.A., 17, 18, 19, 34, 98, 99, 101, 105, 111
Cooper, Edwin, 18, 24
Cotman, John Joseph, 19, 47, 48, 52
Cotman, John Sell, 11, 18, 19, 21, 22, 23, 27, 28, 29, 32, 35, 38, 39, 41, 43, 47, 48, 49, 51, 52, 57, 58, 59, 61, 63, 66, 67, 69, 70, 72, 74, 75, 79, 81, 82, 83, 85, 89, 91, 93, 94, 95, 96, 99, 100, 102, 104, 105
Cotman, Miles Edmund, 19, 43, 47, 48, 52
Cox, David, 39, 104
Crome, John the Elder, 18, 19, 20, 22, 23, 24, 28, 29, 35, 49, 50, 56, 57, 59, 61, 62, 63, 69, 91, 93, 98, 99, 100, 102, 104, 105
Crome, John Berney, 19, 24, 43, 51, 52
Crome, William Henry, 19, 21

Day, Harold, 44, 106
Daniell, Rev. E.T., 23, 56, 57
Dixon, Robert, 18, 22, 23, 38, 50, 57, 101, 102

Gainsborough, Thomas, 19, 98, 99, 102, 104, 105
Girtin, Thomas, 21, 27, 61, 67, 96, 99, 100, 102, 103, 104, 108

Hardie, Martin, 32
Hemingway, Andrew, 102
Hitchens, Ivon, 32
Hodgson, Charles, 18, 19, 59
Hodgson, David, 51, 102

Kitson, Sidney, 67, 69, 70

Ladbroke, Robert, 18, 19, 20, 22, 23, 24, 59, 91, 98
Ladbroke, Fred, 19
Ladbroke, Henry, 19, 22, 29, 32, 58
Ladbroke, John Berney, 19, 20, 24, 32, 35, 44, 58, 102, 104
Leman, Robert, 41, 43, 57, 58, 69, 101, 104
Lound, Thomas, 19, 24, 39, 41, 43, 44, 52, 101, 104

Margitson, Maria, 24
Middleton, John, 19, 20, 24, 43, 44, 46, 59, 104
Monro, Dr. Thomas, 63, 67, 87, 92, 100
Moore, Andrew, 72, 81
Munn, Paul Sandby, 61, 67

Ninham, Henry, 38, 51, 101, 102

Norwich Castle Museum, 27, 48, 49, 59, 81, 91, 92
Norwich Mercury, 21, 28, 69
Norwich School of Painters, 12, 17, 18, 21, 23, 24, 27, 38, 39, 44, 49, 57, 59, 61, 63, 87, 97, 98, 103, 105, 106, 108
Norwich Society, 17, 18, 19, 20, 21, 22, 24, 27, 28, 47

Oppé, A.P., 72, 102

Pleasance, Geoffrey, 96

Reynolds, Graham, 72, 100

Sandys, Antony, 59
Sillett, James, 18, 24
Sillett, Emma, 24
Squirrell, Leonard, R.W.S., R.E., 4, 9, 10, 11, 12, 17, 21, 24, 27, 30, 32, 44, 48, 49, 51, 52, 57, 59, 61, 62, 63, 66, 69, 72, 74, 75, 79, 81, 82, 83, 86, 88, 89, 90, 91, 93, 94, 95, 96, 98, 100, 102, 103, 104, 105, 106, 108
Stannard, Alfred, 23
Stannard, Eloise Harriet, 24
Stannard, Joseph, 19, 20, 22, 23, 50, 56, 58, 102
Stark, James, 18, 20, 22, 23, 32, 34, 35, 39, 51, 99, 102

Thirtle, John, 18, 22, 27, 28, 29, 30, 32, 39, 52, 56, 57, 89, 91, 92, 101, 102
Thomas, Denis, 41, 43, 70, 92
Tonks, Professor, 10, 63, 100
Turner, Dawson, 22, 70, 75
Turner, J.M.W., 19, 61, 67, 96, 99, 100, 101, 103, 104

Vincent, George, 19, 22, 23, 35, 99

Ward, Vernon, 11